Die Riß.

DREAM
TOWNS
OF EUROPE

DREAM TOWNS
OF EUROPE

Joseph Wechsberg

Weidenfeld and Nicolson London

For George

Designed by Tim Higgins
for George Weidenfeld and Nicolson Limited
11 St John's Hill, London SW11

ISBN 0 297 77195 7

Printed in Great Britain by
Butler & Tanner Limited, Frome and London

CONTENTS

ACKNOWLEDGMENTS

Illustrations are supplied by or reproduced by kind permission
of the following (*numbers in italics indicate colour illustrations*):

Alinari 112
Almasy 32, 51 (both), 54, 55
By courtesy of the Austrian National Tourist Office 138, 145, 146
Bath City Council 10, 13
B. T. Batsford 107, 116
Bavaria-Verlag 68, 72, 74, *75*, *76* (above), 77, 87, 91, *96*, 97
Anne Bolt 2, 156
Belgian National Tourist Office 154
British Tourist Authority 17, 20, 22
Camera Press 37, 40, 41, 70, 85, *95*, *126* (below), *166*, 171, 173
Country Life 21, 29
Douglas Dickens 64, 81, 83, 86, 89, 90, 92, *126* (above), *150*, 157, 177, 178
Robert Estall *45*, *58* (above)
Feature-pix 160, *168* (above), 174
Foto-Archief de Porceleyne Fles 164 (both), 165
French Government Tourist Office 34, 38, 53
Mrs E. L. Green-Armytage 14, 15
Michael Holford *26*
Italian State Tourist Office 102
A. F. Kersting 31, 33, 99, 100, 101 (left), 117 (left) *121*, 159
Mansell Collection 63, 67, 73 (both), 110, 113
Mas 133, 134, 135 (both), 136
Sheila Orme 18
Picturepoint Ltd *25*, 27 (both), *28*, *46* (below), *57*, 149, *168* (below)
Pictor International Ltd *76* (below), *78*
Popperfoto 42 (both), 69, 105, 108, 119, 120, 127, 141, 142, 152, 153, 155, 163
Scala *122* (below), *122–3*
Ronald Sheridan 23, *46–7*, *47* (below), *48*, 50
Edwin Smith 101 (right), 114, 117 (right), 118
Spanish National Tourist Office 128, 131
Swiss National Tourist Office *58* (below), *61*, *62*

Picture research by Annette Brown
Map drawn by Jennifer Johnson

FOREWORD

EVERYBODY HAS DREAMS, but no two dreams are alike. When I selected my own dream towns of Europe, I expected my selection to be called arbitrary, even bizarre. I made it mainly on the basis of what I personally like. My dream towns are not supposed to be the dream 'cities' of Europe, the famous places where anybody who wants to be somebody must have been at least once in his life. Venice, the dream of millions of people, is a dream city. Nearby Verona, though known to many, is still a dream town for people who love old legends and old buildings, the sound of music and the sound of the past.

A dream town may be large but it remains a town rather than a city. Paris is the super dream city but the Île Saint-Louis, hidden in the very heart of Paris, remains a dream town. A dream town is not just one more stop on the international jet route. It is not for people who often can't remember what day it is nor where they happen to be.

We dream town folk know exactly where we are and why we go there. We don't mind when our dream towns have no airport, not even a railway station. We go there by car or by bus. Our dream towns are not hard to find, but we may have to get off the main route, off the *autobahn*. Sometimes, if we are lucky, we discover the old charm of a quaint, deserted country road.

Consequently this book is not a travel guide, written from folders and pamphlets. You may still want to consult your Guide Michelin, Baedeker, or Egon Ronay's Dunlop Guide. I won't tell you how to get there, how much it will cost, what to eat or where to stay, not to mention where to get another repair job on the car. Rather, this book will help you decide *whether* to go there in the first place. I'll do this by giving you the facts and my own enthusiasm. I'm not trying to persuade you. I leave the persuasion to your husband, or your wife and her mother, to travel agents and members of your chess club who offer a convenient low-fare arrangement for twenty-five or fifty people. None of that.

My dream towns are personal discoveries, though I won't claim to be the first to discover them. The discovery may range from landscape to legend, from a good meal to a picturesque inn, and almost always interesting people will be included, wonderful lunatics who can be found in these places if you know how to look for them.

It's not always beauty or sightseeing I'm after. Rather it's a hidden beauty, something I like and want to share. Yes, to share my own likes with my readers – that is the purpose of this book.

J.W.

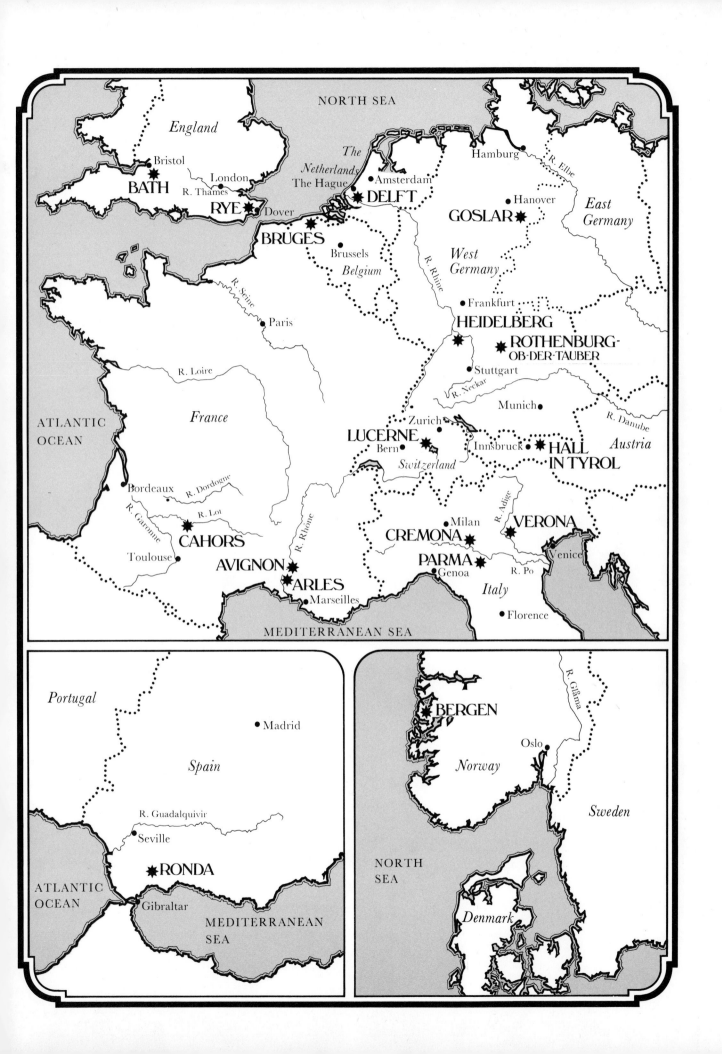

BATH
Somerset, England

BATH IS NOW FAMOUS for its Roman baths and its near-perfect Georgian architecture, but the legend of Bath begins long before the Roman invasion. In the eighth century BC, according to the medieval chronicler Geoffrey of Monmouth, King Hudibras ruled over a kingdom reaching from Cornwall to the Cotswolds. Alas, his son Bladud got leprosy, became an 'outcast' and had to leave his country. All he took was a ring his mother gave him. Bladud found a job as a swine-herd near Keynsham, by the Avon. Naturally, in no time the pigs caught leprosy from Bladud, who took his herd into the woods until he reached Swine's-wick, possibly today's Swainswick. There the pigs would wallow in the nearby hot springs and black mud. Soon Bladud noticed that the pigs lost the symptoms of leprosy. Incredulous – so the legend goes – he tried the treatment himself, taking a hot mud bath every day. After a week or so, he was cured.

Bladud took his pigs back to Keynsham and from there went to his father's court where they didn't recognize him until he showed his mother's ring. In due time, Prince Bladud became king after the death of his father and built his new capital at Caer Badon, the city of baths. Some called it Caer Yrn Naint Twymin, the city of the warm valley. Anyway, it was Bath, and today Bladud has two statues there, at King's Bath and at Cross Bath. He was even featured during the 'Thousand Years of Monarchy' celebrations in Bath in 1973. Not bad for a legendary hero who may never have existed.

It is certain though that people lived near Bath before the Romans arrived and built their baths. They dedicated them to the goddess Minerva but wisely also gave credit to the British goddess Sul and named the place Aquae Sulis, the waters of Sul. The Romans built their palaces and baths of a locally available, oolitic white stone which after many years takes on a cream-coloured or golden hue, especially when sunlight falls on it. Archaeologically, Bath remains a challenge since later towns were superimposed on the older Roman foundations. Underneath the streets of Bath is a network of cellars and crypts, and the Roman ruins remain ten to fifteen feet below the present ground level. On top of them the Saxons built their town, using stones from the Roman ruins. The medieval builders demolished the Saxon houses to put up *their* town, and then came the Georgian master builders whose Bath we now admire as a priceless jewel of urban architecture. The

The Roman Baths, a piece of Roman Britain: lead from the Roman mines in the Mendips covers the floors and Roman-built ducts still convey unused water to the River Avon.

experts have wistfully speculated how fine it would be to put the whole town on pillars and open to the tourists the subterranean crypts with their remains of the Roman era.

The Roman baths, excavated with great care and understanding, are a splendid sight. There is the eighty-foot-long central bath, probably uncovered as it is now, surrounded by cloisters and ante-chambers where the bathers were given special hot and cold plunges, then known as *caldaria* and *tepidaria*. There are the pillars on which the floors were built, the water channels, stone steps and Corinthian columns. In the nearby museum one sees coffins, coins and tools. With a little imagination one feels like waiting to see Roman gentlemen in togas come in to ambulate, converse and bathe.

The Roman legions left around 410 AD but their families often remained and there was a Roman–British population. Quite a few legionnaires may have deserted and stayed behind. It is possible that Bath was Mount Badon where King Arthur defeated the Saxons. But the Saxons stayed on, having little use for the Roman establishment. After a while the 'white city' became a ghost town and a collection of ruins. Fortunately Bath was situated on the Fosse Way, the Roman-built highway between Lincoln and the south coast near Seaton. The road section between Bath and Cirencester was called the Akeman Street. And Akemanceaster was the Saxon's name for Bath. Around 676 AD the grant of land near Bath to an Abbess Bertana was recorded; a nunnery was built, and a small church was erected near the hot springs that later became the Abbey.

In 973, King Edgar 'The Peaceful' was crowned at Bath, probably on the advice of St Dunstan, Archbishop of Canterbury. The coronation was attended by many priests 'and a goodly company of monks and wise men gathered together', according to the *Anglo-Saxon Chronicle*. (One thousand years later, in 1973, Bath celebrated the anniversary with pomp and pageantry.) The event made such an impression on the populace that they decided to hold an annual election of a 'King of Bath' at Whitsuntide. Not much happened until 1012 when Sweyn, King of Denmark, decided to set up his headquarters at Bath. In the eleventh century Edward 'The Confessor' married Edith, daughter of the Earl of Wessex, who owned all of Bath that wasn't held by the Abbey. Edith eventually went into a nunnery but King Edward, no fool, kept her property, and ever since there has been the division between royal and ecclesiastical landlords in Bath. Later John of Tours, Bishop of Wells, moved his diocese to Bath and built a new Abbey on the site of the former one. From 1090 to 1218 Bath had a bishop's church and a Bishop of Bath and Wells. Bishop John ordered the Roman baths restored and added two more, one for public use. 'Sick persons from all over England' came to bathe 'in the healing waters'.

In the sixteenth century the Norman church was pulled down and a new Abbey in the elegant perpendicular style was built, smaller than the former one, but beautiful with a fine square tower. The chancel vaults at Bath Abbey, made by the great William and Robert Vertue, are a masterpiece, noble and very English. Many people feel that walking through the Abbey with the light coming through the branch-like tracery is like walking through a wooded glade in the countryside.

Bath's most elegant example of Regency architecture is Royal Crescent, part of which has been restored, due to the efforts of the Bath Preservation Trust, and is now open to the public.

After Henry VIII dissolved the monasteries, a city corporation took over much of Bath and appointed a Keeper of the Baths who paid for the privilege. Bath became very well known; around the middle of the seventeenth century bottled water from Bath was used all over England against all sorts of sicknesses. In 1576 a new bath for women had been added, which became known as the Queen's Bath, but it was later demolished to give access to the Roman bath located directly underneath. In the late seventeenth century Bath became popular with kings and queens. Among the early visitors was Samuel Pepys, who noted that the baths were 'pleasant, and the manner pretty enough, only methinks it cannot be clean to go so many bodies together in the same water'. Other diarists wrote that the water was changed twice a day. Everything was very strict and decorous. Women had to wear yellow canvas gowns while bathing. When they got out, a woman attendant would throw 'a flannel garment' over their heads and 'strip off the wet costume underneath', and then the ladies were put in

enclosed chairs and carried off to their bedrooms. The sybaritic Romans
would have blinked. There were tennis courts, bowling greens and pleasant
walks by the river Avon.

And there were gambling places. In fact, the eighteenth-century prosperity of Bath started with gambling rather than bathing. Members of the
landed gentry arrived, allegedly for the purpose of taking the waters, but,
to tell the truth, actually to have a good time gambling with congenial
friends. A popular gambler was that gentleman of fortune, Richard Nash,
who came to Bath in 1705, three years after Queen Anne had given the
place her approval. Nash was the son of a glass manufacturer in Swansea,
had been to Oxford and got a commission in the Guards, but he preferred the high life in Bath, the company of attractive women, and the
gambling places. He was also a sartorial wonder, always impeccably
dressed. His income came from gambling. Eventually he became Master
of Ceremonies, an unpaid position that gave him much power in Bath.
(Once he was even elected 'King of Bath' for a year.) He was the local
arbiter elegantiarum, deciding who was in and who remained out, and once
told a princess, 'I reign here and my laws must be kept.'

The intricate ironwork (right) *seems a direct contrast to the very regular Palladian architecture of Bath Street* (opposite) *but in fact is just as symmetrical.*

Nash was a benevolent despot, though, and he did much for Bath. He ordered the Old Pump Room, two theatres, a cold bath room, the fine Assembly Room, and a ballroom to be built. At that point John Wood arrived in Bath. He was a builder, architect, amateur historian and a man of imagination. His grand idea was to restore Bath to its former, Roman splendour, to make a white city again, more beautiful than the one that had been there. The style of Palladian classicism had been brought to England from Italy in the early seventeenth century by Inigo Jones. In Bath, Italian Renaissance became refined by English understatement; surprisingly this worked beautifully. The British made Italy's noble classicism very intimate, very English; it is wrong to call Bath 'the Florence of the North'; it wouldn't be fair to either city. The Georgian style is simple and elegant. All houses have the same width and height (three stories). The simple windows are almost functionally set into the façade. The middle story is the *piano nobile* (or *bel étage*), just a little more prominent. There is a minimum of columns and architraves and few ornaments.

John Wood began in 1724, working on various projects at the same time. It is not known whether he had an overall blueprint for Bath. After his

Bath

death in 1754–at the age of only forty-nine–his son, John Wood the younger, continued the work. He died in 1775 but by that time the dream had come true: Bath was a white city, more beautiful than the Roman town, with no break in style. It is perhaps England's most elegant town. Spacious streets, secluded squares; the Royal Crescent, a half-moon-shaped complex of thirty houses with 114 Ionic columns, looking down from a hill on to a park; the Circus, round and formed by houses with no steep roofs or gables; Pulteney Bridge, with rows of small shops, and the Holborne of Menstrie Museum, once the Sydney Hotel, one of the finest houses in England; even the small streets, Queen Street, Beau Street, Cheap Street and Gay Street have the unmistakable flavour of Bath's *belle époque*. Bath was the rendezvous of everyone who was anyone. Memorial plaques commemorate the famous people who came to Bath: Oliver Goldsmith, Jane Austen, Gainsborough, Haydn, Macaulay, Thackeray, Fielding, and Dr Johnson, to mention a few. The guest-lists of the eighteenth century were a veritable who's who of England of the period.

By the end of Bath's great century, it had become somewhat *démodé*. George III preferred to spend much time at Cheltenham, and George IV went to Brighton. Bath expanded in size and population, the Great Western Railway linked it with London, the water supply and a sewerage system were installed, schools and hotels, hospitals and libraries were built, but Bath became a museum. It is still elegant and popular with tourists but remains something of a museum nevertheless. Today Bath is an industrial city with a resident population of almost 85,000 people, home of the American Museum (with exhibits relating to eighteenth- and nineteenth-century America), the Victorian Art Gallery, a modern university opened in 1966 and a research institute of the Admiralty. At Popjoy's, the elegant restaurant in Beau Nash House, Kenneth Bell, chef-proprietor of Thornbury Castle, Avon, and one of the best cooks in England, offers an antique-style dining room and refined, modern cooking.

But Bath is not a young town, and many residents are elderly people. Their town has problems that didn't worry the Woods, father and son. The town is set in a narrow valley and there are traffic jams. Bath still attracts people who like to step from the Roman baths, almost two thousand years ago, to the sixteenth-century Abbey nearby, and from there to modern department stores. The dream is almost too good to be true, and the controversy goes on. Should the demolition of some of the charming Georgian houses be permitted to make space for a twentieth-century concrete-and-glass skyscraper? Or should Bath remain a jewel of the past, one of the very few places in Europe where the heritage of the past has been faithfully preserved?

The palatial north façade of Queens Square which was built by John Wood in 1734 and named after Queen Caroline.

RYE
Sussex, England

HENRY JAMES CALLED RYE'the very calmest and yet cheerfullest that I could have dreamed', and lovingly described it as 'the little old, cobble-stoned, grass-grown, red-roofed town, on the summit of its mildly pyramidal hill and close to its noble old church – the chimes of which will sound sweet in my goodly old red-walled garden'. The description is both poetic and accurate. Henry James came to Rye, Sussex, in 1897. The tourists had not yet discovered the place, and Rye was quiet and quaint, and quite genuine. James came often in summer and sometimes in winter too until he died in 1916. His friends from America came to see him, and so did G.K.Chesterton, H.G.Wells and many other writers. Henry James liked to work in the garden room of the Lamb House, where he would leave the window open, and people could hear his deep, strong voice; he was probably dictating to his secretary.

Lamb House was named after the Lamb family, once powerful in Rye. At one time a Lamb was mayor and his two sons were magistrates. Such things happen everywhere. Eventually that seemed too much though, and in 1825 the freemen of Rye met secretly at the old cross in the town's church-yard, the traditional voting place, elected their own mayor and occupied the Guildhall. There they stayed for six weeks, but in the end the Lambs had them thrown out and were back in power. The last of them, a Dr Lamb, Rector of Iden, Playden and East Guldeford, a rather arrogant parson, died in 1864. He had been five times mayor. E.F.Benson lived for many years in Lamb House and wrote many books in the garden room where once Henry James had worked.

These days in summer the cobbled streets are crowded with vacationers and tourists, sometimes so many of them that a few old Ryers prefer to stay at home. The wonder is that the medieval charm of Rye persists; apparently it is too strong to be spoiled. And people who have been there once, often go back. Rye does that to people, perhaps because the Old Town inside the wall has hardly changed. That cannot be said of Hastings or Battle where William the Conqueror in 1066 rewrote England's history. Hastings Castle is a noble ruin. People go to Bodiam to see a fine old fortified English castle. A visitor from the sixteenth century who came to Rye today would easily find his way around town. Not many places can make such a claim.

Historians are not certain about the beginnings of Rye. Once the manor of Rameslege (or Rameslie) controlled much of the shore between Hastings

Lamb House, built in 1722; the garden room, where Henry James often worked, was destroyed by bombs during the Second World War.

19

and Rye. Ethelred the Unready, in exile in France, promised the region to the abbey of Fécamp, should he ever be restored to his throne. This happened, whereupon he conveniently forgot his promise. Later his widow persuaded her second husband, Canute, to give the region to Fécamp, and William the Conqueror confirmed it. After his victory he punished many districts and noblemen that had been against him, but he touched neither Rameslege nor the fishing village of Rhie or La Rie. The name may come from the French *rie*, 'a bank of the sea', or from the Old English expression meaning 'at the island'.

Rye supported the successors of William in their efforts to keep hold of their French possessions. This was a dangerous policy. In 1339 some sixty French ships attacked Rye and burned more than fifty houses until an English fleet crossed the Channel and set fire to Boulogne. Located on a hill and fortified, Rye was a challenge and a power. Henry III exempted the Barons of Rye from the payment of revenues, provided they would use the money to keep the walls in good repair as there was always the chance

A picturesque scene along the Rye marshes.

of floods and occasionally armed invaders. When Henry III ordered the castle at Hastings to be restored, he said that any funds left should be used to build a castle in Rye. Only a tower was built in 1249, and in 1430 Rye, in need of money, sold it to John de Ypres after whom Ypres Tower is now named. Another version, unconfirmed, claims it was built as early as 1135 by William de Ypres, a Norman nobleman.

It was first used as a watchtower, commanding a fine view of the shore, Romney Marsh, and the hills near Folkestone and Dover. Nowadays the view includes the atomic power station at Dungeness. Ypres Tower was at various times a prison and a mortuary; now it is a museum. Underneath is the Gungarden (the Battery), where some old cannons were placed prior to the First World War. After the war a few old field guns were put there, but all guns were removed at the beginning of the Second World War. It was feared they might make Rye look like a fortified town and thereby provoke the Germans. The attempt at détente failed, and the Germans bombed Rye, hit the top of Ypres Tower and destroyed and damaged some houses. In the final months of the war, Rye found itself in the path of the v-1 flying bombs.

Rye became used to violence during its earlier days. It does look like a fortress, and the thick wall around it protected it against its enemies. One of the old gates, known as the Landgate, is still there and delights amateur photographers. It is an impressive structure with drum towers and a clock in its arch that was installed much later. In 1377 Rye was invaded by the French, who used it as a base for making forays into the countryside. The abbot of Battle collected some fighting men and set up headquarters at nearby Winchelsea. (Its medieval church of St Thomas the Martyr has some twelfth-century tombs.) At that the French plundered Rye and took the church bells, set fire to the town and sailed home. The following year, the angry Ryers and fighting men from Winchelsea invaded Normandy, where they looted churches, set fire to Dieppe, and, best of all, brought home the bells of Rye. An impressive *quid pro quo*.

RIGHT *Now a museum, Ypres Tower has served the people of Rye as a watchtower, a prison and a mortuary ; the walls linking the Tower to Land Gate have been destroyed by sea erosion.*

In Rye local pride and a sense of independence were strong, and every man wanted to be a freeman. In Rye they prayed, 'God save Englonde and the Towne of Rye', according to the Rye Customal of 1564. Actually the 'usages' were older. The preamble said they were used 'of tyme out of mynde whiche mens myndes cannot think to the contrary'. Rye had proud sailors, merchants, craftsmen, and also gunmen and smugglers. They were not narrow-minded and accepted the Huguenot refugees from France after the St Bartholomew's Eve massacre (1572) when almost fifteen hundred sought asylum; and again in 1685 after Louis xiv foolishly revoked the Edict of Nantes and many able people fled the country. A few local families have French-sounding names, and the influence of the new settlers has been traced on the façades of some houses. The immigrants were generally made welcome, since they replaced the many victims of the plague, but sometimes there were too many guests and there was trouble. Some became quite active, among them a certain Cornelys Shier, a sharp operator who bought up all supplies of candles and hired other immigrants to make more candles. Eventually he monopolized the entire candle trade and dictated the prices. A formal complaint was made to the Lord Warden of the Cinque Ports and Shier's practice was stopped, but the affair caused much bitterness.

After storms diverted the river Rother from neighbouring New Romney to the foot of the cliff of Rye, vessels could land there and trade flourished. But eventually Rye shared the fate of New Romney as silt accumulated in the bay and much of the river disappeared, and with it the prosperous trade. In the early nineteenth century there was still water in the bay. The fields were flooded and then the silt increased, and now the fields are known as the Town Salts. Rye is now almost two miles from the sea but many people no longer deplore this. They are convinced that Rye would have lost its medieval appearance long ago if the developers had taken over; they say things are bad enough in Cinque Ports Street and its vicinity. Only the walled Old Town remains as it was.

The oldtimers in Rye remember wistfully that once their town was as popular with painters as it is now with amateur photographers. The painters were often amateurs too. Henry James writes about 'a train of English and American lady pupils' who came to study with some painters, who told them to put up their easels at certain picturesque points and afterward made their rounds among the disciples. 'There are ancient doorsteps which are used for their convenience of view and where the fond proprietor going and coming has to pick his way over paraphernalia, or to take flying leaps over industry and genius.'

One of Rye's best-known attractions is the Mermaid Inn in steep, cobbled, often crowded Mermaid Street in the heart of the Old Town. The *Guide Michelin* mentions its 'fifteenth century' past but Ronay's *Dunlop Guide* is more specific: 'One of the oldest inns in England, this half-timbered building was rebuilt in 1420 after a fire. It has had connections in the past with smugglers and fugitive priests.' As the inn grew, it absorbed some neighbouring houses, and now the interiors are a marvellous confusion of creaking stairways and narrow, winding passages on changing floor levels. Some bedrooms have four-poster beds and private bathrooms, 'many in odd shapes and sizes'. The public rooms have such attractions as oak beams, linenfold panelling and wall paintings.

Once the place really was a smugglers' haunt. William Holloway, noted local historian, writes of a man born in Rye in 1740 who had seen members of the Hawkhurst gang 'seated at the windows of this house, carousing and smoking their pipes, with their loaded pistols lying on the table before them, no magistrate daring to interfere with them'. For a long time there was no inn at the place, and only around the turn of the century did the Mermaid become a licensed club and finally a hotel with a good restaurant.

Two other houses in Mermaid Street are interesting. The older one was built in the sixteenth century and called the Old Hospital after the Napoleonic wars. On the other side is the house Samuel Jeake started building in 1689, adding a sign inset with the astrological situation at the time he laid the foundation stone. Jeake apparently lived by the stars. They told him to marry a girl of thirteen, and he did. The stars didn't lie: it was a good marriage.

The Hope and Anchor Hotel in Watchbell Street dates 'only' from the seventeenth century and features a Jacobean staircase, low-ceilinged bedrooms and 'a fine view of marshland, river and sea'. Watchbell Street took its name from the warning device housed there. It seems to have been used a lot, for the bell rope had to be renewed quite often, and records exist to prove it. The Flushing Inn Restaurant dates from the fifteenth century. When the place was restored in 1905, a well preserved wall-painting (1544)

Mermaid Street and the sign above the famous Mermaid Inn which backs on to Mermaid Passage, an old resort for highwaymen and smugglers.

FOLLOWING PAGES
LEFT *The Roman Baths.*
OPPOSITE ABOVE *The symmetry of the architecture and ironwork of Bath's Regency Crescent is stunning in its simplicity.*
OPPOSITE BELOW *Built between 1769–74 by Robert Adam, Pulteney Bridge spans the Avon, connecting Bath with Bathwick.*

ABOVE *A quiet corner of the church-yard at Rye.*
LEFT *Rye's cobbled Church Corner and the house with the crooked chimney.*

was discovered behind the panelling of the main restaurant. On another occasion one James Breads, butcher of Rye, was permitted to have a last drink there before he was executed. He'd had an argument with the mayor, and murdered a man whom he believed to be the mayor, but it was all a ghastly mistake.

And there is old St Mary's Church, with a nice Elizabethan clock on the northern side, flanked by two quarter-boys with hammer, or, more exactly, by a boy and a girl. Originally made of wood, they have now been replaced by duplicates made of fibreglass. At fifteen minutes past the hour they strike one stroke each. Between the figures is an inscription, 'For our time is a very shadow that passeth away'. When the pendulum inside the church was repaired years ago, people were shocked to discover that it was hanging by one nail and might have fallen on the congregation.

In the churchyard the freemen of Rye customarily met at an old cross to nominate and elect their new mayor. He might of course refuse the nomination, but if he did he ran a certain risk because the rules said that 'the whole commons together shall go beat down his chief tenement'. Under the circumstances, even a reluctant nominee might feel it wise to accept.

ARLES
Bouches-du-Rhône, France

P LACE DE LA RÉPUBLIQUE IN ARLES is a dream square in a dream town. There a visitor in a hurry – and most visitors are in a great hurry nowadays – may comfortably walk within minutes through thousands of years. The oldest exhibit is the Egyptian obelisk, surrounded by a fountain made of Roman stones. Nearby is the great Romanesque Church of Saint-Trophime with beautiful sculptures of the Last Judgement and the Apostles on the western portal (truly a masterpiece), with a fine twelfth-century cloister. The cloister's sculptures and columns make it perhaps the most beautiful in Provence. The severe and particular architecture of the cloister is seen in the region in many variations, but rarely as beautiful as in Arles. Later the Maltesian Order built several buildings nearby that now contain the Musée Réattu. Saint Trophime, first bishop of Arles, is said to have been sent into Provence by Saint Peter.

That would be sufficient for half a dozen squares, but in Arles it is only the beginning. There is the Musée d'Art Chrétien (Early Christian Art) at the old Jesuit School. A short distance away is the Roman Forum, and nearby is the Museon Arlaten that the great poet, Frédéric Mistral, endowed with the money from his Nobel Prize. The late-Gothic Church Sainte-Anne, nineteenth-century houses, and late twentieth-century stores, bicycles and automobiles complete the illusion of several civilizations in a nutshell.

All this and more is Arles, population 46,000 people, sous-préfecture in the *département* of Bouches-du-Rhône. Once a Celtic–Ligurian settlement, Phoenician and Greek trading post, and colony of the veterans of the Sixth Roman Legion who fought for Julius Caesar and Augustus, the Colonia Julia Paterna Arelate Sextanorum has been the residence of Roman emperors Constantine III and Majorianus. The Romans made their Arelata the second capital of their empire and, believing in *panem et circenses*, they built the theatre of Augustus, the amphitheatre, the *cryptoporticus* under the Forum and the thermal baths of Constantine.

No less than nineteen Church Councils took place in Arles, many dealing with the momentous problems of the early Christians. The West Goths under Eurich, and later the East Goths and the Franks, swept through. Burgundy's rulers were crowned in Arles, as rex Burgundiae, rex Alamannorum et Provinciae, or rex Arelate. (In 1178 AD Frederick I

The Church of Saint-Trophime was founded in the seventh century but was rebuilt several times thereafter, making it essentially a Romanesque structure.

30

Arles

Barbarossa was crowned at the Church of Saint-Trophime as rex Arelate.)
That all happened before Arles became a Free City and was eventually
subdued by Charles of Anjou and became part of France.

In Arles one is easily confused unless one knows a little history. Many
know nothing about it, but they enjoy the sunshine and the air and the
colours, and possibly *la course à la cocarde*, a bullfight at the arena. They
too enjoy Arles though they are ignorant of its complex history. Arles is a
Mediterranean melting pot, filled with Algerians, Moroccans, gypsies,
tourists, French bureaucrats, monks and fascinating locals, chewing cold
cigarette butts and wearing berets. It must be a great place for painters.
Greatest of all was the strange Dutchman Vincent van Gogh, who was here
in 1889. Arles may have looked to him almost as it does today. Van Gogh's
cell at the former cloister of Saint Paul de Mausole was shown for many
years after his death to awed visitors, with faded reproductions of his works
on the walls.

Nothing seems to matter very much in Arles, least of all time, which has
no meaning locally. Generations of builders – amateurs and pros, pagans and

ABOVE LEFT *A detailed view of the
arches around the amphitheatre built by
Emperor Hadrian and still in use
today ; originally there were three levels
of arches but only two, with sixty
arches each, remain.*
ABOVE *Since the fifth century* BC
*Arles' Roman Theatre has served as a
quarry for churches, walls and houses ;
consequently, only its outer walls and
splendid marble columns remain.*

monks, rulers and burghers – would use the stones of earlier buildings when
they put up their churches, palaces or houses. Arles is much loved by the
people who live there, who say they wouldn't want to live elsewhere, that
Arles has 'almost everything'. It has the right size, they say, neither too
small nor too large. It is located on the banks of a great river, the Rhône,
in a beautiful region with a warm climate. There is the mistral, to be sure,
and it can be very windy in Arles, but nothing is perfect. Nearby are the
strange, dark mountains of Provence that seem to have a strange attraction
for fanatics and cultists. Unlike Avignon, often called an 'Italian' town, Arles
makes you think of Spain, with its bright lights, very dark shadows, and
silent streets ascending towards les Arenes.

Colourful cruelty was always plentiful at the arena built by Emperor
Hadrian in the second century and enlarged two hundred years later by
Emperor Constantine. In principle nothing has changed at the arena.
There was and is the thrill of violent death: once the Roman gladiators
fought against wild animals while the people cheered; and now celebrated
bullfighters risk their lives to kill the bulls, and the twenty-one thousand

The ancient cloisters of Saint-Trophime are reputedly the most beautiful in Provence.

spectators are probably as excited as the Romans were almost two thousand years ago.

'Here one can truly say, "*plus ça change ...*",' an Arlésien said the other day:

Life and death are very close in Arles. It is no accident that Georges Bizet, who was not a Spaniard but wrote a very Spanish opera, also caught the music of our region in his *L'Arlésienne*. We have everything here, the Rond-Point des Arènes, the rue Voltaire, the rue de la Republique, the rue du President Wilson, and the avenue Stalingrad. We are all things to all men.

At the nearby necropolis of Les Alyscamps is the once-pagan burial ground lined with Roman sarcophagi. The most beautiful of them were presents which the thoughtful rulers of Arles gave to their friends – after which they might have their friends killed to make sure they wound up in the right sarcophagi. The early Christians were not buried in the modern manner. Instead their families would put the dead bodies into boats on the Rhône, always putting some coins near the bodies for those who found them. Pious monks would get hold of the boats and bury the dead. Gradually Les Alyscamps became an early Christian cemetery. If the dead were lucky, they were buried in the vicinity of the grave of Saint Trophime, who had originally been buried at the Church of Saint Honorat.

In the Middle Ages, the Roman necropolis was transferred to the Benedictine Abbey of Montmajour in the vicinity of Arles. There the Chapel of Saint Pierre was hewn out of the rocks, probably at the time of the Carolingians. They also built the eleventh-century Notre-Dame Church and added a cloister a century later. But in 1786 Louis XVI abolished the abbey. The abbot, who happened to be Cardinal de Rohan, had been involved in the mysterious affair of the necklace of Queen Marie Antoinette. Some of the ruins have since been restored. The Chapel Saint Croix en Jerusalem is on the battlefield where Charlemagne is said to have defeated the Saracens. Arles wasn't just another old town – it was a kingdom, and later a rich republic, and the people were anxious to build things for eternity.

During the summer when Arles is often hot and windy the old town is crowded with visitors. Most of them are so eager to take pictures of the fine sights that they have no time to think of the distant past. Arles thus remains truly a place for all seasons. Ausonius called it 'Gallula Roma', the little Rome of the Gauls. Arles still looks that way.

CAHORS
Lot, France

I N SOUTH-WESTERN FRANCE, half-way between Avignon and Bordeaux
and still overlooked by the organizers of mass tourism, is the *departe-*
ment of the Lot in the ancient province of Quercy. Its administrative
capital is the medieval town of Cahors, with a population of only 20,900
inhabitants, though it is crowded and noisy enough on weekends when the
people of the vicinity come for shopping, gossip and entertainment. The
river Lot flows around the old town on its way towards Bordeaux. Nearby
is the region called Le Périgord, with its prehistoric caves, Romanesque-
Byzantine churches, old buildings and old bridges, and with some of the
world's best truffles, fine *foie gras* and dark, earthy wine. The main river,
the Dordogne, is beloved of fishermen, campers, and visitors of old castles.
Château de Fénelon, named after François de Salignac de la Mothe-Fénelon,
the poet born there in 1651, was built as a fortress in the fourteenth century,
although today it boasts a swimming pool.

Also in the area are Château de Montfort, high up on a rocky cliff above
the Dordogne, Château de Latreyne and Château de Belcastel, surrounded
by dark woods. The sixteenth-century Château de Beynac has been beautifully restored. Château de Montal is a jewel of pure style. In between are
sleepy, ancient villages where the houses are made of unpainted grey stone
and the roofs are masterpieces of curved orange tiles. Time seems miraculously
to have stopped in some corners of the region.

The strange mystical fortress of Rocamadour, in the heart of the Quercy,
is perhaps the oldest pilgrimage town in France. Its basilica, chapels and
old houses are almost welded to the rocks, and at the top is the castle. There
is a strong medieval mood about the place, a spell that even the new hotels,
son et lumière on summer nights, and Jean Lurçat's modern tapestry at the
town hall reception room cannot destroy. One senses the religious past, the
mystique of the Black Virgin despite the floodlights trying to improve a
landscape which needs no improving. And there is excitement of a different
kind at Gouffre de Padirac, where an underground river winds through
huge eroded caverns covered with enormous stalactites (hanging down from
the roof) and stalagmites (rising from the floor). Between Easter and late
October one can take a boat ride, three hundred feet below the ground,
which is worth the trip through the region.

Cahors is the centre of this strange, little-known part of France. Like many
other reluctant dream towns, Cahors is reticent and withdrawn, not eager

*Extensive industrial development has
bypassed Cahors and it has changed
little from medieval times, as
can be seen by the picturesque rue
Château du Roi.*

*The Pont Valentré, with three machicolated towers
like the one pictured here, is reputed to be
the finest remaining fortified bridge in France.*

to offer its treasures; one has to search for them. The Romanesque Cathedral Saint-Etienne, built by Bishop Géraud de Cardaillac in the late eleventh century on the site of a much older church, is a magnificent building; the cloister was added in the sixteenth century. The most famous structure, Pont Valentré, also known as Pont du Diable, The Devil's Bridge, is the finest Romanesque bridge in France, with three towers resting in the river. It was conceived in 1308 as a military bulwark when Cahors was on the frontier between the possessions of the king of France and the Black Prince. It is still solid and strong today, almost seven hundred years later. According to a legend, the builder was so worried by the slow progress of the work that he signed a pact with the devil and lost his soul to Satan. But that legend is not restricted to Cahors: when the master builder Hanns Puchspaum worked on the southern tower of St Stephen's in Vienna, he fell in love with Maria, the daughter of his boss, Hans von Prachatitz. He asked for permission to marry Maria and was told to come back when he had built both towers at the same time. This was obviously impossible. Puchspaum too signed a pact with the devil – and lost. Though he later died peacefully, it is a nice story.

Quercy and Périgord are among the oldest civilized regions in Europe. In prehistoric times Cro-Magnon Man lived in the caves of Lascaux and Les Eysies de Tayrac. The local theory is that prehistoric men elected to live there, as well as along the Dordogne and in the valleys of the Lot, because the landscape was beautiful and the land generous. The northern part, close to the town of Périgueux, is called Le Périgord *vert*, for its green meadows. Farther south is Le Périgord *noir*, because of its dark oak trees. Black truffles grow there, those mysterious diamonds of *la grande cuisine* that have been known to connoisseurs for thousands of years. Beautiful small villages have resisted progress: at La Roque Cageac, built into the very rocks surrounding it, one can see the ancient troglodyte habitations dug out of the rocks. Domme, the once heavily fortified village high on a promontory, is where some of the most grim religious wars of the Middle Ages were fought.

In the small town of Sarlat, called the capital of the black Périgord, the houses of the ancient heart of the town have been restored in the past ten years with knowledge, skill and devotion to detail. The whole *quartier* is a delight. In summertime the old streets are artfully floodlit. I saw them in wintertime when they were dark and deserted, and very beautiful still. There is a summer festival in the Place de l'Hôtel de Ville; apparently the tourists' appetite for festivals is insatiable. On Saturday mornings between November and January a famous market is held in the square. *Foie gras* and truffles, morels and *cèpes* (mushrooms), geese and game, and fine beef from Limousin are offered and bought. One is always surprised at these modestly-dressed Frenchwomen, certainly not rich, who select carefully, know what they want, and pay a lot of money for the good things.

This is a country for archaeologists, historians and gastronomers. Jean Secret, president of the Société Historique et Archéologique of Périgord, wrote the preface to a well-documented study by Henri Deffarges, *L'Histoire du Foie Gras*, followed by *La Truffe et son Mystère à travers les Ages*. In France it is considered perfectly proper for an historian and archaeologist to be also a full-fledged gourmet. M. Deffarges proves that prehistoric man knew and appreciated geese and truffles. Statuettes and stone sculptures depicting geese have been found in the caves of the Dordogne. Apparently the goose was highly thought of by the prehistoric cave dwellers before it became known in China, India, Persia, Assyria and Egypt. The British Museum has an Egyptian bas-relief showing two herds of geese. The Louvre has a bas-relief with wild ducks that was found in ancient Memphis. There can be no doubt either that the Egyptians knew the culinary delights of *foie gras*. In the *Odyssey*, Homer mentions 'a goose fed in the mansion of Menelaos'.

The sybarites of Rome loved *foie gras*. Emperor Heliogabal, who regaled his guests with the tongues of nightingales and the heads of peacocks (he was said to be crazy) also gave them goose liver, which doesn't seem crazy, just expensive. Juvenal and Martial both report that everybody in Rome who could afford it loved *foie gras*; it is rare that a satirist and a poet agree on anything. M. Deffarges, a man of diplomatic ability, doesn't expressly state whether *foie gras* as we know it was first created in Périgord or in the region of Strasbourg (each region makes the claim), but there are no statues of geese in prehistoric caves in Alsace. Maybe *that* is the answer. Actually *foie gras*, a delicacy known all over the world, has been made during the past two hundred years both in Périgord and in Alsace.

Truffles, which remain the leading gastronomic mystery as so little is known about them, come from Périgord and Lot, and from a few other

The fifteenth-century guardhouse, La Barbacane, forms part of the medieval defensive structure to the north of Cahors.

The hexagonal Renaissance tower of the Collège Pélegri was a defensive stronghold in the fourteenth century; it includes a fine spiral staircase which can be seen on request.

Founded in 1119 the Cathedral of
Saint-Etienne dominates the old town
and was the first church in France
to have these Byzantine-style
cupolas (below).

regions in France, but none from Alsace, so the Strasbourg manufac-
turers must buy their truffles elsewhere. Roman epicures loved black
truffles two thousand years ago, but today the wise men in Cahors and
Périgueux admit that they know very little about 'the jewels of French
cuisine'. (The white truffles of Piedmont in Italy are different in texture and
aroma, much loved in Italy and very expensive, but some experts in
Périgord don't consider them truffles at all.)

During the truffle season, from November until early March, the truffle
market in Cahors is held every Saturday morning in Allée Fénelon, on one
side of the large square that is filled with parked cars. A few trees give the
impression of an 'alley'. Rugged-looking peasants with almost prehistoric
faces and black-clad women, severe and unsmiling, stand around with
covered shopping bags and straw baskets, presumably filled with fresh
truffles. They are suspicious and won't show their jewels until they have
heard about prices, supplies and the economic facts of truffle life.

Truffles are best known as the black spots in fine *foie gras*. They grow in
the soil, sometimes fifteen inches below the surface, often in the vicinity of
oak trees that become known as *chênes truffiers*, 'truffle oaks'. Truffles grow
but cannot be grown. Optimistic farmers plant oak trees. If they are lucky,
they may have truffles twenty years later. The nineteenth-century agrono-
mist, Comte Pierre de Gasparin, would say, 'The trick is to sow acorns of
truffle oaks in the right soil', which is like saying put your money on Number
29 at roulette in Monte Carlo before 29 comes out. Truffles have no
roots, no leaves. They seem to be formed – no one is really certain – by a
mysterious symbiosis near the roots of the trees that probably furnish the
carbohydrates. They can be as small as a Boston bean or as large as an Idaho
potato. All this sounds vague, but it is all the scientists know. No one is able
to explain why a truffle ground – a few truffle oaks – may yield a fortune one
year and not a single truffle the next. The truffles are sniffed out by specially
trained small pigs or dogs that smell the truffle hidden deeply in the
ground. Demand always outruns supply. Next to caviar, truffles are the
costliest delicacy on earth.

In Cahors they showed me a man who had made 'thousands of new francs'
last year on his truffle ground and 'not a sou' this year. He is said to be
drinking, and no wonder. Many farmers get discouraged waiting for truffles,
and plant vines or fruit trees; they won't get rich, but at least they won't
starve. In the past quite a few packed up and went away to work in the cities.
Prior to the First World War, over 400,000 people lived in Périgord and Lot.
Now only some 150,000 remain. In 1900 the Dordogne area produced one
hundred and fifty tons of truffles; last year it produced ten tons. The buyers
in the Cahors market either work on their own account or for a large firm.
They know that the farmers don't trust them; the farmers accept 100-franc
notes but never a 500-franc note. They claim to have been burned.

The biggest truffle market is held in a small village, Lalabenque, fifteen
miles from Cahors, population 876 last year. It takes place every Tuesday
afternoon during the harvest, and has to be seen to be believed. Under a
primitive corrugated-iron shed that is open on all sides, men and women
stand holding their tightly-covered baskets. The shed is surrounded by open

Cahors

trucks with new washing machines, refrigerators and agricultural machines. It was raining when I was there, but that bothered neither the peasants nor the refrigerator salesmen. When a farmer sold his truffles, he might walk over to the trucks, with the 100-franc bills still in his fist, and buy a new washing machine or whatever else he needed. There might be an economic lesson in this, but I am not sure, since the farmer might never again find truffles on his ground – or he may find many more tomorrow. Statisticians who like their facts neat and clear wouldn't like the truffle business. Exactly at two pm the market opened, and for a while there was the excitement of bids made, rejected, raised, turned down, and so on, that one knows from stock market dealings and auctions. Forty minutes later it was all over, and three thousand kilos of 'black diamonds' had changed hands at $70 a kilo. By the time you buy the truffles in an elegant store, they'll cost perhaps twice as much. A good place to taste the strong aroma of fresh truffles is La Taverne in Cahors, the best restaurant in the region, which Pierre Escorbiac set up in 1952 in the former headquarters of the local fire brigade. A wise and witty man, he loves his region and its specialities, and he sings the praises of the *vin du pays*, the wine of Cahors.

Edward III called it 'the black wine of Cahors'. It remains one of the least known tips on the large French wine market. Its history is an almost uninterrupted chain of disaster. The vines were brought into Lot by the Romans until Emperor Domitian ordered half the vineyards to be destroyed and decreed that grain must be produced instead. Under the Emperor Probus new vines were planted; Probus was later killed by his drunken soldiers and became the patron saint of vintners. In the seventh century the Bishop of Verdun thanked the Bishop of Cahors for 'the noble Falerne', a great compliment which compared Cahors wine with wine from southern Italy that had been praised by Horace and Vergil.

Later the wine of Cahors had no chance against the wines of nearby Bordeaux, though it was sometimes sent to England and to Russia. Peter the Great drank *Caorskoie vino* for his stomach ulcer; we don't know whether the treatment was successful. Next Cahors wines faced the competition of cheap *vin du Midi*, and in 1877 phylloxera reached Quercy and wiped out half the vineyards. That was bad, and worse was to come. Between 1910 and 1932 black rot and mildew ruined several harvests, and then large imports from Algeria began. Algerian wines 'blended well' with Midi wines. By 1950 production of *vin de Cahors* was down to 1500 hectolitres.

Today that figure has doubled and is increasing. The blackest of all French wines, with a strong *goût de terroir* (taste of the soil), *vin de Cahors* is slowly becoming more popular, thanks to such enthusiasts as Henri Laborde, an aristocrat from Lot whose wife is Queen Margrethe II of Denmark. When Comte Henri Marie André Laborde de Monpezat became Prince Henrik of Denmark, it was a lucky break for the black wine of Cahors.

The Pont Valentré, Cahors.

FOLLOWING PAGES
ABOVE *A charming panoramic view of Arles.*
BELOW LEFT *Excavation begun in the seventeenth century at Arles' Roman Theatre has yielded numerous art objects.*
BELOW RIGHT *The cloisters of Saint-Trophime, Arles.*

AVIGNON
Vaucluse, France

ALL OVER THE WORLD the sophisticated French run schools, called *lycées*, where foreign children are taught the beauty of the French language and the glory of French civilization so they'll never forget. It's first-rate cultural propaganda. Among the first things they learn is to sing '*Sur le pont d'Avignon, l'on-y-dance, l'on-y-dance....*' I've always liked that song, which conveys a dream. Elsewhere children learn lullabies or Christmas carols, or silly 'patriotic' songs. At the *lycée* they sing about that wonderful, faraway bridge where people don't walk, but dance. A fairytale bridge in Avignon. Where's Avignon? The boys and girls don't know and they don't care; perhaps it's the dance capital of the world. I thought so myself for a good many years, until I came to Avignon and was told that people never danced on the Pont Saint-Bénézet but rather underneath the stone arches, where they enjoyed the shade, on the Île de la Barthelasse.

The bridge was no disappointment when I at last saw it. A fine Romanesque structure, according to legend it was built between 1177 and 1185 by the famous builder, Saint-Bénézet. Twenty-two powerful arches stretched across the wide, wild Rhône. But one night the high waters of the river tore down and broke off pieces of the structure. Only four arches survive, four out of twenty-two, and the bridge now breaks off in the middle of nowhere. What can be done with such a noble torso? Leave it for the tourists, who take innumerable photographs. It really belongs, with *Winged Victory* and the *Venus de Milo*, at the Louvre, with what the French call '*mutilations heureuses*'. To restore the bridge would be as foolish as putting arms on the statue of Venus or completing Schubert's *Unfinished Symphony*. Anyway, the Rhône is no longer a wild, unpredictable river. It has been tamed and forms part of the great European waterway, the Rhône–Rhine axis, that will connect Rotterdam with Marseille, the North Sea with the Mediterranean.

The French still call Avignon the 'city of the popes' because it became in 1309 the capital of the Catholic world. The king of France, Philippe le Bel, forced the politically weak Pope Clemens V to move from Rome to Avignon. Clemens V was a French pope, born in Gascony. It was convenient for the king to have the pope in France, under his close influence. Four popes, among them Benedict XII and Clemens VI, built and enlarged the *Palais des Papes* in Avignon, from 1336 to 1364, into a powerful and

The Bridge of Saint-Bénézet, better known as le pont d'Avignon.

49

Avignon

frightening structure that was a fortress as well as a residence. Nearby stands a Romanesque twelfth-century cathedral, Notre-Dame-des-Doms. After the popes returned to Rome there were anti-popes in Avignon for the next twenty-seven years, when during the Great Schism French and Italian factions chose different popes.

Avignon prospered while the popes resided there 'in Babylonian captivity'. The town acquired twenty-seven monasteries, fifteen convents, seven hospitals and seven cemeteries. The popes turned the town into an impregnable fortress with massive towers and strong gates, ten-foot-wide walls and machicolated battlements. (The walls were later restored by Viollet-le-Duc.) Rabelais, born in Chinon, in the Loire district, called the fortified town of Avignon '*la ville sonnante*' because there was almost always the sound of church bells. At that time, over a hundred thousand people lived below the Rocher des Doms. Some of them probably danced underneath the bridge. After the French Revolution when the *Palais des Papes* was badly damaged, only 17,000 people remained. Today Avignon has 89,000 inhabitants, but the atmosphere of history is strong. People walk quietly along the old walls under the birch trees, and the mood is timeless and peaceful.

The famous *Palais des Papes*, Avignon's chief attraction, now seems less a residential palace than a prison, a sinister fortress where the popes must

In the shadow of the Palais des Papes are houses and churches which date from the sixteenth and seventeenth centuries.

An imposing façade of the Palais des Papes; the citadel of the Avignon popes is one of the largest châteaux-forts still in existence, with walls 13 feet thick and 150 feet high.

From 1818–1906 the Palais des Papes was used as an army barracks; almost all the decoration was supposedly removed by the soldiers who chipped the plaster from the frescoes in order to sell it.

have felt like prisoners themselves. There are labyrinths of corridors leading to empty vaulted rooms, cold and unfriendly even on a hot summer day. Some parts of the palace are impressive: the *Vieux Palais* has its cloister tower, and the *salle de grande audience*, built under Clemens VI, is noteworthy. The Pope's bedroom, known as *chambre de cerf*, is decorated with beautiful frescoes painted by Simone Martini. But the frescoes and works of art fail to dispel the sense of gloom which remains in the dark corridors that sometimes end rather suddenly and abruptly, like one-way streets. This is in fact what some of them were, designed to lure and trap potential assassins who might get lost there and be caught by the armed guards. The popes knew better than to trust anyone. Even honoured guests might be murderers in disguise. Harmless visitors sometimes turned out to be dangerous terrorists. History shows that nothing is new; and the fact that we never learn from it isn't new either.

There are several stairways leading directly down to and into the Rhône. Perhaps they were built for people who wanted to get away in a hurry. They were also used when certain people were to be drowned at night, while no one looked on. Avignon was much feared during the Middle Ages, when feuds and intrigues often ended in terror or torture. Dante accused the high and the mighty of misusing their power, but no one listened. Francesco Petrarch came to Avignon as a young man but became so terrified that he left 'Babylon' and sought refuge in the peaceful valleys of the Vaucluse. There he lived with his beloved poets of the Antique and wrote his sonnets for the eternally beloved Laura.

The people of Avignon feel nostalgic pride about the great era under the popes, when their town was full of artists and ladies of doubtful morals, poets and plebeians, painters and murderers, lobbyists and wheeler-dealers. Some made the best of 'captivity'. Pope John XXII created chairs for the study of Hebrew, Arab and Chaldaean at the universities of Bologna, Oxford, Paris and Salamanca. And in 1334 Benedict XII asked Petrarch to go to Rome and prepare the pope's return. Poor Petrarch dutifully went there but the ruling families of Rome, involved in their feuds, had no use for the pope. They received the poet and appreciated his sonnets, but that was all he could do. They even decorated the poet with a wreath of laurels; they had good manners and knew that poets love wreaths of laurels. Petrarcha deposited the wreath at the high altar of St Peter's. That was the end of his mission.

In 1343 Cola di Rienzo, last of the tribunes, went to Avignon to try to convince the pope that it was high time to return to Rome. There he got involved in the feud between the Orsinis and Colonnas, and was killed on the stairs of the Capitol. Mary Russell Mitford wrote a drama about it, Bulwer Lytton wrote a novel, and Richard Wagner wrote both the text and the music of his opera *Rienzi*. Then Catharine of Siena managed to get Pope Gregory XI out of Avignon-Babylon and back into the pope's palace near St Peter's in Rome. In 1377 the pope entered St Peter's. During the Schism there were two, and sometimes three popes, until Amadeus of Savoy, known as Pope Felix V, retired to the serene tranquillity of the Lake of Geneva. It was an interesting time and some people in Avignon wish it

had never ended. It gave Avignon fine churches, the Carthusian monastery at Villeneuve-les-Avignon, and the Cistercian abbey of St Bernard's.

Avignon is located in that strange, sunlit land of dark legends and mystical past known as Provence. The word is derived from the former *Provincia Romana*. It is the land of the troubadours, of Frédéric Mistral. Roman monuments and medieval secrets are all over Provence. There is the strange ghost town of Les Baux where Raymond de Turenne amused himself by having his prisoners thrown from the battlements of his castle into the dark abyss below. The coat of arms of the rulers of Les Baux shows a mysterious sun with sixteen rays. In 1632 Louis XIII was so upset by the strange and sinister tales of Les Baux that he ordered his troops to attack and destroy the town. Today the ruins of the former aristocratic buildings are more impressive than the houses of people living there. In Les Baux-de-Provence, a short ride from Avignon, is one of the great restaurants of

Descending through the Rocher des Doms, the garden of the cathedral, one comes upon this peaceful view of the Pont d'Avignon

France, Oustau de Baumanière, a creation of the astonishing Raymond Thuilier, painter, poet, builder and great chef. A fascinating place in a fascinating region. Van Gogh lived in nearby Saint-Rémy-de-Provence, and Michel de Nostredame, better known as Nostradamus, once lived in Salon-de-Provence. It's a fine country for murderers and mystics: the unforgotten Marquis de Sade lived in Lacoste; his neighbour, Baron d'Oppède, once had a whole village murdered. Albert Camus, whose fine writings have distressed millions of people, lived in Lourmarin on the southern slope of the Lubéron, 'the mountain of Scorpio', and is buried there. Not far away is the cemetery of Peypin d'Aigues, dominated by a black pyramid. One could go on and on. Today the followers of many well-known and lesser known sects – among them Swamis, Yogis and Zen-

With its landscape dominated by a fortress boasting ramparts and turrets Avignon, with its legendary bridge, still resembles a medieval town.

Buddhists – live in the Vaucluse near the 'holy' mountains of Provence. These mountains rise from east to west, like medieval cathedrals: Mont Vedoux, Ventoux, Sainte-Baume.

Mysticism, and Roman monuments. A strange Madonna at Villeneuve-les-Avignon is crowned by two figures of Christ. Within relatively short distances from Avignon are the Roman theatre and the great Arch of Triumph at Orange; the arena, the Roman baths and the *Maison Carrée* in Nîmes; Arles with its arena, Roman burial grounds and sarcophagi; the Roman ruins in Vaison-la-Romaine, with old churches and old houses; the ruins and cenotaphs of Glanum, near Saint-Rémy. There are many other splendid sights. One can spend weeks in Provence, exploring the distant past, seeing beautiful landscape and eating very well.

In the summer of 1947, Jean Vilar – then thirty-five and not yet famous – brought a group of actors from Paris to Avignon where he knew some people, being a native of nearby Sète. The *Avignonnais* thought this was just another theatrical *troupe* from Paris, bringing the somewhat *passé* hits of the previous

The ornate façade of L'Hôtel des Monnaies, built as the papal mint in 1610, is now the academy of music; the steeple of the church Saint-Agricol rises on the left.

boulevard season to the 'artistically underdeveloped' provinces. Little did they know that Vilar came to Avignon to create something new. He rehearsed for several weeks, preparing the first French performance of Shakespeare's *Richard II* and the world premieres of Paul Claudel's *Tobias et Sara* and of Maurice Clavel's *Terrasse de Midi*. For his open-air theatre he selected the late-Gothic courtyard of the *Palais des Papes*. He used the enormous façade with its asymmetric windows as the back of the stage. This was a long time before summer festivals became unashamedly commercial enterprises. France then had nothing that might even try to compete with Bayreuth or Salzburg or Glyndebourne.

Vilar had the right idea. He wanted to create exciting theatre under the hot sky of Provence for a non-elitist audience, mostly local people who had never been in a regular theatre and might not care for it. But the palace courtyard was different. They liked the place. It was almost like a soccer game in southern France or a bullfight in Spain. It was something that appealed to the local people.

Jean Vilar had a small budget but unlimited energy and boundless enthusiasm. He was carpenter and electrician as well as actor and producer. He didn't call his enterprise a 'festival' but named it *'une semaine du théâtre'*, and it ran from the fourth to the tenth of September. There were about four hundred people in the average audience. Yet Vilar and his TNP (*Théâtre National Populaire*) became one of the truly important institutions of the French post-war stage. The Festival d'Avignon was the first new venture that dared break away from the tired routine of many Paris theatres.

Until he died in 1971, Vilar continued to provide the French stage with powerful impulses. He retained the management of the Festival, which was extended and now lasts over a whole month, offering stage works, ballet (often under Béjart), new films and conferences. In 1968 Avignon presented its Living Theatre. Once Picasso showed some of his works at the *Palais des Papes*. Enthusiasts came from all over the world. But somehow the Avignon Festival has managed to avoid the dangers of fame and the pitfalls of snobbism. Many people in the audience are still from Avignon and from the Midi; Avignon remains a festival for everybody.

Vilar often said later that he hadn't realized what he'd started. Provence is an ideal place for festivals: dry, hot summers so the management needn't worry about the weather and having to cancel performances; Roman theatres and old arenas whose upkeep is relatively inexpensive. Best of all, there is a certain atmosphere built-in and ever-present, which doesn't have to be laboriously created; it is there. In Aix-en-Provence the symbiosis of Mozart's music and of Cézanne's colours thrives in the baroque courtyard of the former archbishop's *palais*. In Orange, the Théâtre Antique was ideal for *Comédie Française* performances, ballet and fine opera. The magic of Provence – old ruins and medieval mysticism, warm evenings and people who instinctively love beauty – is the perfect festival setting.

The Spreuer Bridge over the River Reuss, Lucerne.

LUCERNE
Luzern, Switzerland

Along Lucerne's waterfront.

OPPOSITE *Lucerne's unusually beautiful Musegg Towers.*

THE INCLUSION OF LUCERNE among dream towns of Europe may seem a calculated risk. The tourist who comes to Lucerne in summer will be jostled by hordes of other tourists, and he must wait his turn to buy a picture postcard, a watch, a souvenir or a *café-crème*. He will stand in line to get on a lake boat or to buy a concert ticket. If he is particularly unlucky the *Föhn* will be strong, the dreaded wind that affects people with both high and low blood pressure. Or it may be raining, the sad, steady rain that seems to have a depressing effect on people and landscape. Never again, the visitor will say, as he leaves.

But if you come to Lucerne on a cool, quiet day in late fall or early spring, you'll see the contours of the mountains sharply drawn against the blue sky and the sun reflected in the dark waters of the lovely Vierwaldstättersee, the Lake of Four Cantons. There are no tourists then and you have time to study the paintings on the roof portions of the fourteenth-century covered Chapel Bridge, showing scenes from Lucerne's history and from the lives of its patron saints, Leodegar and Maurice. You'll sense the magic of the Old Town (*Altstadt*) with its narrow lanes, fine houses and palatial homes once built by patricians but used now by councils and assemblies. There is a colourful atmosphere that one doesn't often feel in Switzerland, a sober matter-of-fact country excelling in hotels, watches, chocolate and cheeses. But Lucerne has a solid quality – a rugged past, conservative confidence and quiet pride – qualities that have disappeared in many parts of the world and which make this beautiful picturesque town surrounded by mountains and water a sort of dream that does not exist elsewhere. It takes a long time to make a friend in Lucerne, but a friend there is a friend for life. Do not expect charm, however. The Swiss have a first-rate currency and William Tell (whose likeness has been sanctified on the five-franc coin), but they wouldn't know how to spell charm in any of their four official languages.

The historians don't agree on the origin or the name of Lucerne. The name may come from St Leodegar, or from the word *lux* (light). An ancient legend tells of a small chapel dedicated to St Nicholas, patron saint of boatmen. One night people along the shore saw a radiant glow above the chapel and called the place 'Luzern'. Today the Stiftskirche stands on the site. There are many churches in Lucerne, perhaps because the commanders

Lucerne

of the Papal Swiss Guard were citizens of the town for centuries. Today Lucerne is synonymous with 'light' to people who see the town at night from the mountaintops that surround it. I've watched the lights many times from the Bürgenstock – a mountain that remains the private property of one man. Fritz Frey, owner, police chief and fire chief, holds all authority there and produces his own electric current. Only the long-distance telephone and the post office do not belong to him. From this late-capitalistic enclave of feudal property the lights of Lucerne at night seem like a string of blue-white or white-blue diamonds. No accident perhaps, since the firm of Gübelin, ranking with the great jewellers of the world, has its home office in Lucerne.

In the thirteenth century a bridge was built across the Schöllenen Gorge at the foot of the Gotthard Pass, and Lucerne became a stopping-place and trading station for merchants from the north and south of Europe; for a while Lucerne hoped it might become the rival of Milan. But the people of Lucerne have never had the ambition to become rich and powerful. It may have been their enjoyment of the good things in life, or perhaps the *Föhn*. Some historians disapprovingly call Lucerne a place of missed opportunities that never took full advantage of its geographic location. 'The spirit of Italy was so strong above the Gotthard that the parties in Lucerne fought as in Florence or Pisa,' writes Ricarda Huch. Luzerners played an important part in the belligerent history of early Switzerland; they were always present when there was a battle or at least a solid fight. A popular legend tells of a brawl at night after which sixteen *Ratsherren* (councillors) had to be carried away dead.

When the Luzerners didn't beat each other up, they ran their excellent inns and hotels. Lucerne was a fashionable place where my parents went and their parents before them. Around the turn of the century it was chic for the so-called moneyed classes to be seen in Lucerne. The large Grand Hotel National, that takes up a considerable section of the lake shore, was managed by one César Ritz and its *chef de cuisine* was a certain Auguste Escoffier. Their names have since become bywords of luxury and gastronomy. The best suites were usually occupied by kings and maharajahs, milords and millionaires. Old photographs exist which are beautifully amusing. The great hotel is still there, wearing a white-elephant look. Today's *Sozialtouristen* don't stop at luxury hotels; they don't care for palm trees in lobbies. They would rather take a plane and look at real, wild palm trees. In Lucerne the tourists appear in the morning, spilled out by large buses, and dutifully absolve their 'programme', having no time for meditation or improvisation even if they wanted it, and late in the afternoon they pile back into their buses and depart; whether or where they sleep, I have no way of knowing.

In spite of all this Lucerne has kept a straight face and unspoiled character. It accepts all comers but hasn't sold its civic soul to mass tourism. The town has managed to make the difficult switch from the rich-and-privileged to the new class of travellers in shorts and shirt-sleeves and remains Lucerne, with its old towers and patrician houses, covered wooden bridges and churches surrounded by glorious landscape. On a quiet day late in October the population may actually be 75,000 but two months

A rooftop view, from the old city walls, of the town's romantic spires.

earlier, during the 'season', it seemed more like a quarter of a million, give or take 20,000. Fortunately you don't see them all, since a good many are busy going up and down mountains in cable cars or taking a ride on the nice white lake steamers.

That's fine with the people of Lucerne. They listen to the sounds of their cash registers, even more pleasant than those of the cowbells, and quietly go about their business. The tourists leave no mark on the community. They come, modern locusts, spend their money and are gone again. Other dream towns have been hopelessly spoiled, but Lucerne goes through the annual April-to-October commotion apparently with eyes and ears half-closed. Luzerners who can afford it go away. But when the evenings become dark and lights go on early, the people of Lucerne are back, happily involved in city or canton (state) politics, not very much interested in the world outside the Lake of the Four Cantons. They cannot ignore the sad facts of recession or the decline of dollar and pound, because many of their favourite guests, Americans and English, no longer come or if they do, spend much less money. But the Luzerners, being close to history, have learned patience.

On a nearby mountain meadow, the Rütli, the Swiss democracy was formed on 1 August 1291 by a number of mountaineers from the nearby

Lucerne

Urkantone Schwyz, Uri and Unterwalden. The canton of Lucerne joined them very early, in 1332. The sense of history remains strong in Lucerne but many things are changing, though the changes are not always visible. A growing number of *Eidgenossen* (Confederates) have learned the awful truth about William Tell who–according to the cherished legend long accepted as truth–shot the evil Landvogt Gessler in Hohle Gasse in Küssnacht (just a short ride away) and thus started the revolt against the Habsburgs who, ironically, had originally come from Switzerland. But today many Swiss know that the Tell saga was probably imported from Scandinavia, where master archers amused themselves by shooting apples from the heads of their loved ones long before 1291. The Swiss owe their legendary hero to the German playwright Friedrich Schiller, who wrote his beautiful drama *Wilhelm Tell* without ever having been to Switzerland. Well-educated, modern Swiss know that the real revolutionaries were the men of the large 'radical' cantons that forced the smaller 'conservative' cantons to accept the Confederacy in 1847. 'Yet eighty-four per cent of all twenty-year-old Swiss know the "revolutionaries" of 1291 but only eleven per cent know the revolutionaries of 1847,' writes Otto Marchi, the Lucerne-borne historian and journalist. Still, the Swiss are lucky to have Tell, on and off the five-franc coin. In quiet times Tell remains the symbol of Swiss freedom and perhaps of law-and-order; in times of violence, Tell is an early revolutionary. He is a man of all political seasons, everybody's hero. A great many countries on all continents would be glad to have a national hero like William Tell.

In Lucerne, located in the very heart of Switzerland, one cannot help being reminded of the past. During two world wars while the world exploded

An orchard overshadowed by Lucerne's medieval ramparts.

The Kapelbrücke, the roofed wooden bridge, houses 111 sixteenth-century paintings depicting the history of Lucerne and its saints; it adjoins the fourteenth-century octagonal Water Tower which once formed part of the town's defences.

outside the borders of peaceful Switzerland, a few fortunate foreigners who belonged to the surviving moneyed classes sat out Armageddon in a luxurious Swiss hotel. The Swiss were no fools: they mobilized their small but excellent army and air force, rationed their food, mined their Alpine frontier passes, and defied potential invaders with 'over our dead bodies'. They made it clear that neutrality was not always a bed of roses and Swiss francs, but also a privilege and always a sacrifice. There was stronger anti-Nazi feeling in the German-speaking parts of Switzerland than in the west and the south, where people speak French and Italian. They succeeded in convincing potential invaders that they meant business. The strategists decided the risk was too big and did not invade. During the Second World War the Swiss had less to eat than people in America, yet today it is fashionable to condemn the Swiss as 'the only country that managed to stay out of wars in modern times', and to blame them for making a nice profit on wars. Who doesn't if he has a chance? The gnomes of Zurich did not invent banking secrecy or numbered accounts. But the Swiss Henri Dunant created the most international institution of all, the Red Cross.

In his *Impressions de voyage* Alexandre Dumas père remembers how he visited Chateaubriand in Lucerne in 1832. Chateaubriand took him to the Lion monument commemorating the last stand and massacre of the Swiss Guards who defended the Tuileries palace of Louis XVI against the

63

revolutionaries on 10 August 1792. Dumas remembered 'with emotion and admiration' how Chateaubriand regretted that 'the blood shed for the monarchy was shed by citizens of a republic'. Nowadays serenades take place in front of the monument during the International Festival of Music, held every year in August and September.

Musical life in Lucerne goes back to the fifteenth century when they had medieval Easter and Passion Plays. The Jesuits employed music as persuasion; during the baroque era, there was much good music in the churches of Lucerne. The Swiss Musical Society was founded there in 1808. In 1858 Richard Wagner wrote the music of the third act of *Tristan und Isolde* in the prosaic atmosphere of the Hotel Schweizerhof in Lucerne. In 1866

Along the river Reuss are many beautiful old squares and burgher's houses.

64

Wagner rented a fine country house in nearby Tribschen and wrote much of *Meistersinger, Siegfried* and some of *Götterdämmerung* there. Othmar Fries, the local historian, wrote that Wagner had little contact with musical life in Lucerne, preferring the company of Gotthard postilion Zgraggen, paper-hanger Aeberli, tailor-master Häcki, coiffeur Stoll, bookbinder Schlapfer, bookseller Press and watchmaker Bossard, but he also saw painter Zelger and music director Arnold. There were prominent guests in Tribschen: Bavarian King Ludwig II 'who paid the expenses of Wagner's expensive household', father-in-law Franz Liszt, conductor Hans von Bülow and Nietzsche, who came twenty-three times. Tribschen is now a Wagner Museum, the Medina of proper Wagnerians who had already visited the Mecca of Bayreuth. Noted contemporary artists – Edwin Fischer, Carl Flesch, Georg Kulenkampff, Rafael Kubelik, Wolfgang Schneiderhan, Irmgard Seefried and others – lived or live in Lucerne. Lucerne was proud to present during the same season the two great antagonists, Furtwängler and Karajan. Perhaps they all feel what Tolstoy during his visit in 1857 called Lucerne's 'strangely exciting and inexpressibly harmonious Nature'.

What to do in the dream town? The guidebooks mention all the local sights: the Chapel Bridge and the Water Tower next to it, once a prison, now the guild house of the Artillery Association; the wooden Gothic Spreuer Bridge, built in 1408 as part of the town's fortifications. Its roof partitions show forty-five paintings of a baroque dance macabre, made around 1630 by Caspar Meglinger and his pupils, commissioned by leading Lucerne families. The patricians did a lot for Lucerne. The Hertensteins hired Hans Holbein to decorate their house, although unfortunately it was pulled down over a century ago. The former Sonnenberg castle became a home for old people. The Town Hall is a fine late-Renaissance building with a Swiss hip roof. Landammann Ritter had a splendid Florentine palazzo built that is now used as a state government building. In the Tuscan-style inner court-yard, Jakob von Wyl painted his version of a dance macabre in 1615. Obviously Switzerland and the Swiss are more complex than they seem to the visiting foreigner.

It is easy to see the interesting things in Lucerne but difficult to find out the secrets behind them, yet it is these secrets that give Lucerne its dream town quality. It is a town of many paradoxes, and it is very Swiss. The Swiss have many beautiful lakes, but none like the Lake of the Four Cantons, synonymous with the birth of the Old Confederation. It was a Luzerner, Colonel Ludwig Pfyffer, who rescued King Charles IX of France from being encircled at Meaux by the Huguenots and was given the name 'King of the Swiss'. Another Luzerner, Landammann Johann Rudolf Dürler, was considered 'the most influential Swiss of his time' by the ambassador of Louis XIV. After Lucerne lost its kings, it discovered the majesty of tourism. But no matter whom they serve, the Luzerners remain always themselves.

GOSLAR
Lower Saxony, West Germany

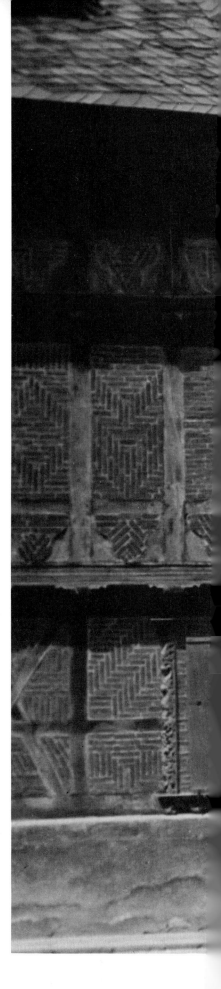

I N THE *Altstadt* (old town district) of Goslar 168 buildings were built
before 1550. Two-thirds of all houses were put up before 1850. Nearly
all are inhabited and well-kept. The people of Goslar know how much
they owe to their unique heritage. Some parts of the former imperial
town have the unreal quality of a stage set, but they are genuine.

Goslar, forty miles north of Göttingen, is somewhat off the beaten path –
even the nearest *Autobahn* is fifteen miles away – but it is worth the trip.
Among the many medieval towns of Germany Goslar is one of the truest
and most beautiful. The Second World War has bypassed it, they say, 'as by
a miracle'. Young Goethe came to Goslar after it had lost its power and
gone to sleep, but he found himself happily 'lost in walls and roofs of
antiquity'. Heine did not find 'the narrow, labyrinthine streets' very attractive; he compared the statues of German emperors on the façade of the Guild
House of the *Gewandschneider* to 'baked proctor's men'. But he admitted he'd
found a pretty girl and kissed 'a beautiful curly head', so the visit was not
a loss after all. Today everything in Goslar is almost as it was – the walls and
roofs of antiquity, the narrow streets, the pretty girls. And in the vicinity are
the beautiful unspoiled mountains and meadows of the Harz, still not as
well known outside Germany as they deserve.

The first mention of Goslar is found in the chronicle of Annalista Saxo,
who claims that '*vicus Goslariae*' was founded in 922 AD. That was good
enough for the citizens, who celebrated their civic millenium in 1922. Originally Goslar was a tiny marketplace that owed its existence to the Rammelsberg south of the town that contained great treasures of silver, copper and
other minerals. Such resources were privileged possessions of the German
emperors, who liked the silver and protected Goslar. Henry II (1002–24),
great-grandson of Henry the Fowler, built his imperial residence, the Pfalz,
in Goslar and set up his court there, probably around 1010. (Pfalz, from the
Latin *palatium*, means 'royal palace'.) The first Pfalz, visible expression of
imperial power in northern Germany, burned down. Henry III and his son,
Henry IV, members of the Salic House, built a new Pfalz which has survived
and is now admired as one of the greatest masterpieces of Romanesque
secular art in Germany, '*clarissimum regni domicilium*'. Henry III was so
devoted to Goslar that he willed his heart be left at the Dome of St Simon
and Judas, across from the Pfalz. In Goslar the church and secular powers
lived side by side for a long time. The Dome was unfortunately torn down

66

Great efforts have been made to preserve the timbered fronts of these beautiful old houses in Goslar.

after 1820, and only its *Vorhalle* (atrium) survives, an exquisite Romanesque structure with fine statuary and imperial throne made of bronze. The heart of Henry III is now kept underneath the Gothic sarcophagus plate in St Ulrich's Chapel, forming part of the Kaiserpfalz.

There, at the largest imperial residence in Germany, much German and sometimes European history was made. The imperial diet was held there, church dignitaries met at synods and ambassadors were received. Emperor Henry III, who carried on a running feud with the popes and deposed three, met there with Pope Victor II.

During the eleventh century, Goslar's greatest era, the emperors put up palatial buildings and fine churches. Henry IV, born in Goslar, installed his governor there. The emperors had awarded the monopoly of the silver and copper trade to the burghers of Goslar, who became rich and wanted to make Goslar a 'jewel' of Germany, sparing no expense. The town must have been a large building site, with many projects financed by either emperors or burghers. Four of the town's churches were built. Goslar had perhaps as many as five thousand inhabitants and was famous throughout Germany. Its power declined, though, when the House of Franconia was succeeded by the Hohenstaufen dynasty. Frederick I Barbarossa held several diets there, but then the production of minerals at the Rammelsberg declined and with it the position of Goslar, though it had been given the privileges of a free Reich city, subject only to the emperor. In 1235 Emperor Frederick II gave the rights to the Rammelsberg mines to the Dukes of Braunschweig-Lüneburg. It turned out to be a fateful decision for Goslar.

The citizens, no fools, realized that only a strong economic position would guarantee them their privileges in future. Late in the thirteenth century they joined the German Hanse. Silver merchants from Goslar travelled as far as Flanders and England. They tried to acquire ownership of the mines and forests, but were unable to buy the rights. The Dukes of Braunschweig would only lease them, and there was always the danger that some day they might take over Rammelsberg with all its installations. In the fourteenth century several flood disasters put the mines out of commission. It took almost a hundred years before experts found new methods to get the mines going again. After 1450 Goslar enjoyed a second silver lining of prosperity. By 1520 there were nineteen mines and twenty-six foundries operating, the mint issued the *Mariengroschen*, and famous breweries had grown up.

Much of what we see now in Goslar was built around that time by rich burghers who liked to live well and loved beautiful things. Most of the older, Romanesque structures were destroyed during the religious wars; only the Kaiserpfalz and a few other places survive. But the civic pride and energetic initiative of the burghers is preserved in the fine buildings they did leave. Among these is the Gothic *Rathaus* (city hall) with its fantastic *Huldigungssaal* (homage hall), beautifully decorated with the paintings of an unknown late-Gothic master on the walls and ceiling. In the large former hall of justice a sixteenth-century fresco was discovered only twenty years ago; it shows the Last Judgement and the painter's grim humour: most of the women are taken by Satan to hell; the men are received by St Peter at the gates of Heaven.

The richly decorated walls and ceiling (below) *are in the Reichssaal in the Kaiserpfaltz* (left) *; founded by Henry II, it is the oldest secular structure in Germany.*

*View from Petersburg through the wooded
Harz mountains to Goslar.*

70

Everyone had money and used it to build in the fifteenth century. A fine Guild House was put up by the *Gewandschneider* (rich men) in 1494, and it survives as the Hotel Kaiserworth, fifty rooms with ninety beds. The fine Brusttuch (the word means 'shawl') was built around 1520 by the wealthy Magister Tilligk, who had made a pile of money at Rammelsberg and commissioned the master carver Simon Stappen from Braunschweig to do the beautiful wood carvings in early Renaissance style. The house has an interesting triangular roof. The Brusttuch is also a hotel with a popular restaurant.

Somewhat older is the Gothic *Bäckergildehaus* (the Guild House of the bakers), today the seat of the Chamber of Industry and Trade. There are many other fine houses in this part of the old town, all with fine woodwork; no wonder, since the nearby forests had all the timber needed. In Goslar it is a joy to study the development of framework houses from early Gothic through the Renaissance to the late baroque. From the house in Marktstrasse One (1526) the way leads to the Siemenshaus, built in 1693 by Hans Siemens, a predecessor of the great inventor and technician Werner von Siemens. Goslar had fifteen thousand inhabitants, and even those who were not rich or patrician had fine houses. It was as if everybody knew it wouldn't last.

It didn't. Though the citizens had fortified the Romanesque walls and put up strong gates, the Dukes of Braunschweig demanded that the Rammelsberg with its installations and forests be turned back to them. The desperate citizens asked the Protestant dukes of the Schmalkaldischer Bund to back them, and joined the league in 1531. After Charles v defeated the Bund in 1547 at Mühlberg, Goslar had to pay a fine of 30,000 guilders and twelve cannons. Five years later Goslar capitulated to Henry the Younger, Duke of Braunschweig, who took over the mines and forges of Rammelsberg and two-thirds of Goslar's forests. Objective historians note that the citizens of Goslar didn't help their cause by burning down several churches outside their town.

Goslar's decline was not apparent at once. There was still great wealth in the town, and many people were employed in the mines and forges. But gradually Goslar was isolated by the growing power of Braunschweig and Hildesheim. During the Thirty Years' War Goslar joined the Catholic Habsburgs, hoping to be rewarded for its unexpected loyalty. But once they had won, the Habsburgs had no use for Goslar. A suit for recovery of the Rammelsberg rights that began in Vienna and continued in Wetzlar was 'adjourned indefinitely'. There began internal feuds between factions of burghers, and tensions arose between burghers and guild members. In 1780 fire destroyed much of the town between Breites Tor and the Market. Goethe, who had noted how pleasing it was to lose oneself in antiquity, also wrote that the former free city 'had decayed in and with its privileges'.

In 1802 Mayor Johann Georg Siemens began to reverse the decline when he reorganized the town's finances and administration. In 1807 Goslar became part of the Kingdom of Westphalia. It had only 5000 inhabitants then, no more than six centuries earlier. The nineteenth century saw the gradual recovery of Goslar's onetime prosperity: new mines were opened at

ABOVE *Such tranquil scenes transport us to another world.*

OPPOSITE *A romantic courtyard with an air of charming intimacy.*

RIGHT *This colonnade bordering the cobbled square is a grand example of the impressive use of timber in the architecture in Goslar.*

Rammelsberg, small industries were started, and in 1866 Goslar became Prussian.

Today Goslar has 41,000 inhabitants and is part of Lower Saxony. Some six hundred people are employed at the Rammelsberg installations that produce two-thirds of all zinc and lead mined in Germany. The only gold found in Germany comes from Goslar. But the citizens seem to have discovered the more prosperous goldmine of tourism. A few years ago the resort place of Hahnenklee-Bockswiese in the Harz became part of Goslar, eight miles away. There Germans who love cures and health resorts go 'once a year'. Goslar is surrounded by old mining towns, ruins of castles, by convents and the beautiful hills and valleys of the Harz. Dream town enthusiasts will love Goslar, and they will use much colour film there.

There is a story of an American millionaire who came to Goslar early in our century and fell in love with its old houses, especially the Brusttuch, said to have the oldest *Stammtisch*, a table reserved for regular guests. It is called *Lange Bank* (long bench) and was installed in 1589. The millionaire, so the story goes, wanted to have the Brusttuch torn down, the pieces sent to America, and have it rebuilt there. The *Lange Bank* would be set up in the United States, and the regulars would be invited for the ceremonial opening. The deal seems to have fallen through – a good thing for Goslar and for America.

Goslar's labyrinthine streets and beautiful architecture are certain tourist attractions.
RIGHT *Goslar's 'walls and roofs of antiquity', which so impressed the young Goethe.*

ROTHENBURG
OB-DER-TAUBER
Bavaria,West Germany

I WENT TO ROTHENBURG on a quiet, cold Sunday in March when the streets were almost empty and its beauty was unspoiled. The tourists hadn't arrived yet and the local people preferred to stay indoors. From somewhere came the sound of churchbells. Dusk fell and the lights went on in their wrought-iron lanterns. The whole town seemed a stage set for the second act of Wagner's *Meistersinger*. Today Rothenburg is close to what medieval Nuremberg may have been. But Nuremberg was badly destroyed in the last war and Rothenburg survived.

Romanticism, a much abused word, still exists in Rothenburg-ob-der-Tauber. 'Ob' means 'on' or 'above', referring to the town's location on a 1300-foot high plateau, 180 feet above the Muschelkalktal, the valley of the Tauber, a tributary of the Main. Its citizens have an admirable sense of beauty and a feeling for traditionalism, and they have been able to keep Rothenburg unspoiled though lately it has been an uphill fight. The town laws preserve Rothenburg's charm and severely limit the citizens' right to change the outside appearance of their houses. Purists have tried to ban all automobiles from the walled, Old Town, which would have helped. Cars don't belong there. Rothenburg is truly a medieval dream town.

Practically the entire old town, surrounded by thirteenth-century walls with roofed ramparts, bastions, portcullis, and beautifully named gates (Gallow Gate, Röder Gate), is classified as a national monument and must remain exactly as it is. A watchdog committee under the *Stadtbaumeister* (Town Builder) controls all repairs and new construction. No ugly skyscraper will be put up on a lot inside the walls. If an old house shows signs of falling to pieces – and some do, with tilting walls and leaking roofs – it must be saved, and if the repairs are prohibitively expensive, the town will come to the aid of the owner. Across from the Town Hall, that has an older Gothic and a less old Renaissance part and baroque arcades, a house is now being repaired. The *Stadtbaumeister*'s office supervises the work on the façade and approves the colour of the paint to be used. Some recently repaired houses were painted in somewhat bright hues, but the experts know the colours will soften in ten or twenty years, and the houses will blend into the medieval ensemble. And what are twenty years in Rothenburg, founded around 900 AD, residence of Konrad of Hohenstaufen in 1137, a Free City since 1172 by decree of Emperor Frederick Barbarossa? In 1400, some six thousand people lived in the walled town,

An unusually quiet scene in Rothenburg – the ancient streets are usually overrun by tourists.

PREVIOUS PAGES
ABOVE LEFT *A view from the Rothenburg tower, overlooking the rooftops and countryside.*
BELOW LEFT *Daily life in 'medieval' Rothenburg.*
RIGHT *Rothenburg's picturesque Old Smithy.*

not very many less than today. Rothenburg doesn't change a great deal.

It is this critical supervision and loving attention to detail that keeps alive the charm of the old town. No ugly neon lights or modern street signs are permitted, no chimneys or posters. The signs and shields in front of inns and stores are made of wrought iron. Progress is limited to the insides of houses. This creates problems: it is expensive to preserve a monument. When Ernst Geissendörfer, graphic artist, art dealer and owner of a fine old house in Marktplatz (Market Square) wanted to install a new printing press, he noticed that the floors of his fourteenth-century house needed support. An architect warned him the repairs might be expensive, say around 100,000 marks.

'By the time we were through, we had taken out practically every wall and rebuilt the whole house inside, keeping the historical façade exactly as it was six hundred years ago,' Geissendörfer says. 'The job cost me 750,000 marks.' For that money he could have built a beautiful modern house elsewhere, but he wouldn't want to live elsewhere. He receives his friends in the cellar that he has turned into a veritable showplace with a large fireplace and a bar. He is a heavy-set, bearded man with a powerful presence who could perform as a member of the *Meistersinger* cast with no make-up. His ancestors have lived in the house for centuries: he traced the family back to 1078 AD and in the process uncovered some long-forgotten, juicy family scandals. One ancestor tried to swindle an emperor and paid for it dearly. Several were mayors of Rothenburg. The mother of Mayor Nusch was a Geissendörfer. Nusch is a legendary figure who saved the town on 31 October 1631 during the Thirty Years' War. General Tilly and his imperial troops had besieged and conquered Rothenburg and issued orders to loot and burn the town and to hang the councillors, which was customary. Mayor Bezold was told to send for the hangman. The women and children went down on their knees asking Tilly to have mercy, and a smart innkeeper offered the general a $3\frac{1}{4}$-litre (almost a gallon) bumper filled with heavy Franconian wine. All right, said Tilly, if one of the councillors would empty the bumper in one draught, Rothenburg would be saved. Nusch, a former mayor, volunteered and is said to have emptied the *Meistertrunk* bumper (which is shown at the local Reichsstadt Museum) in ten minutes. Afterwards, the master drinker slept three days and three nights, and died peacefully thirty-seven years later at the age of eighty.

Connoisseurs of *Frankenwein*, of whom there are many in this part of the country, like the story. The baroque gable of the *Ratsherrntrinkstube* (the City Councillors' Tavern) shows two clocks, one with two windows where at certain hours General Tilly and Mayor Nusch appear and reenact the memorable drinking scene.

In front of the tavern one day in 1474 Emperor Friedrich III sat on his throne and bestowed the title of sovereign of Holstein, Stormarn and Dithmarschen on King Christian of Denmark. In 1525 seventeen rebels of the Peasant Revolt under Florian Geyer were beheaded there by order of, and in the presence of, Markgraf Casimir of Ansbach. A shocked chronicler wrote that 'their blood was running like a brook down the Schmied Lane'. Rothenburg's romantic tranquillity may be deceiving.

Foliage enhances the charm of the quaint medieval buildings along the way to the Röder Arch and St Mark's Tower.

Rothenburg

Nowadays the *Meistertrunk* play is performed once a year at Whitsuntide. On Whitsuntide Monday the 'imperial troops' march from Hospital Gate through the town and the 'soldiers' meet them in front of Gallow Gate, and historic Shepherds' Dances are performed in front of the Town Hall.

Once the Rothenburgers danced around Herterich's Fountain in Marktplatz celebrating the end of an epidemic of the plague or the discovery of a treasure. The fountain has been used since 1446. In 1608 Christoph Körner, a famous local sculptor, built the Renaissance pillar with the statue of St George on top and various coats of arms. The Rothenburg Players occasionally perform farces by Hans Sachs, the sixteenth-century shoemaker-and-poet, and hero of Wagner's *Meistersinger*. Unlike William Tell, who was pure fiction, Hans Sachs did exist.

According to the guidebooks, Rothenburg-ob-der-Tauber has fourteen

To the left of Herterich Fountain is the Marien-Apotheke; in the background, the Gothic Town Hall, built in 1300.

hotels, thirty-five inns and approximately eighty restaurants. Many of the 12,500 inhabitants who live in the historical town or outside the walls in nondescript modern but probably more pleasant homes are working for the tourist trade, now Rothenburg's main source of income. Some people are employed at the AEG plant and in the metal and textile factories nearby. The large AEG façade spoils the view from the old towers but that cannot be helped.

The big question is, how long will Rothenburg be able to preserve its romantic charm? Elderly people remember 'the old days' when the town gates were closed at night and latecomers who wanted to come in had to pay ten pfennig. Some local people are unable to repair their dilapidated houses. Lovely to look at, a photographer's delight, picturesque from the outside, they badly need plumbing and modern improvements inside. There are

Rothenburg

'foreigners' (people living elsewhere) who might be interested in buying an old house in Rothenburg, but they usually back out when they realize how expensive it would be to modernize the inside without spoiling the façade. Several times the more substantial local citizens have had to chip in to provide repairs of old walls and ramparts.

Several years ago Geissendörfer had the brilliant idea of 'selling' the historic wall by the metre. For 498 marks ('sounds better than 500 marks') anyone may purchase one metre of genuine, historic Rothenburg wall and is inscribed in the town books as legal owner. Of course he is not permitted to take away his piece of wall; it stays right there where it always was. But a sign with his name will be fixed to the wall and when he returns with his family or friends, he can show them that he is a proud co-owner of old Rothenburg. Quite a few people have bought pieces of the wall, and their money is used to prolong the life of the historic structure. Retired city councillors donate their time and effort, forming a group called *Arbeitskreis* for the preservation of Rothenburg. This is proof that it can be done if enough people want to do it.

Obviously the Rothenburgers love their town and want to keep it for future generations. It was saved from destruction when the Americans threatened to shell it in the final days of the Second World War because John J. McCloy and other bigshots were Rothenburg fans, and when the town surrendered, it was left untouched in its old beauty. No one seems to mind the present invaders who use American Express cheques, not bullets, and happily leave their money in Rothenburg. A slow walk through the town is almost like a walk through the past – the sort of past we like to think of. Almost each of the patrician houses has an old history and a beautiful façade. Near Herterich Fountain is the Jagstheimer House (now the Marien-Apotheke) with fine framework and a bay window, built in 1488. In 1513 Emperor Maximilian slept there. Next to Geissendörfer's house is the Masterbuilders' House (1596), a fine Renaissance building by Leonard Weidmann, and next to it the fourteenth-century Toppler House. In Herrngasse almost every building has a sign reminding you that some emperor or king stayed there centuries ago. Herrngasse was once known as Herrnmarkt (Gentry's Market); it was the gentry's privilege to keep horses there, and the householders were requested to store supplies and foodstuffs in case of war. At Staudtsches Haus two emperors stayed, Charles V and Ferdinand I, as well as Queen Eleanor of Sweden and the wife of King Gustav Adolph. The house has a beautiful courtyard, galleries and a staircase tower. The fountain in the middle of the street, Herrnbrunnen, was built in 1595. Fountains were important in Rothenburg and the location of the conduits bringing in water from the outside were top secrets, known only to the mayor and the members of the town council. In case of siege an enemy might cut off or poison the town's water supply.

St Jacob's Church is an imposing structure with numerous nuances of Gothic style such as slim windows and tall pillars, built upon the site of a former parish church in 1340 and consecrated in 1448. The southern tower was built by an unknown master, and the somewhat slimmer, taller northern tower by his assistant. When the assistant's tower turned out to be more

This roofed parapet walk projects at the innerside of the second town wall and includes Kummereck Tower and Klingen Gate, built in 1280.

Rothenburg

beautiful, the master jumped to death from his tower. The pointed arcades inside combine the middle nave with the lower aisles. It is the sort of church which makes one look upward, toward heaven. Only a few works of art are there, but they are very fine. At the end of the east choir are three beautiful fourteenth-century stained-glass windows. The great *Zwölfbotenaltar* (Altar of the Twelve Apostles) is a masterpiece made by Friedrich Herlin from Rothenburg, who worked mostly in nearby Nördlingen. A great woodcarver and painter, he also painted the altar wings and the painting showing the dead body of Saint Jacob, with the Rothenburg Town Hall in the background, as it looked before the great fire of 1501.

The greatest treasure inside the church is upstairs, in the Holy Blood Chapel of the west choir, the *Heiligenblutaltar* (Holy Blood Altar) made by the great Tilman Riemenschneider, master carver and sculptor (1455–1531): an unforgettable presentation of the Last Supper. The harmony of the whole is reflected by the perfection of each detail; the Apostles are almost alive and suffering. The golden crucifix contains a rock crystal case with a drop of Christ's blood, a relic admired since the twelfth century. Concerts are played in summer on a fine organ while people sit in front of the Riemenschneider altar. Outside in the Church Square is the former

Rothenburg is the best preserved example of a medieval German town; the Röder Gate, one of several which enclose the Old Town, dates from the thirteenth century.

Rothenburg's double bridge, dating from the fourteenth century, spans the River Tauber and is one of the most interesting bridges in Germany.

Gymnasium building, also created by Weidmann. The beauties of the city are unending. Rothenburg is a jewel.

So is the best local hotel, one of the most picturesque and best run in Germany. The Hotel Eisenhut in Herrngasse has been owned by the same family for three generations. It is a charming and confusing jumble of corridors and staircases on various levels, made up of three former patrician houses artfully joined together. The oldest, now the main entrance, was originally a twelfth-century chapel dedicated to St Nicholas. The Gothic iron door on the left of the reception desk belonged to the chapel. In 1876 Georg Andreas Eisenhut opened a small inn there and sold good wines from his vineyards in the Tauber valley. Today his granddaughter, Frau Georg Pirner, continues the fine tradition. The rooms have old furniture and modern comfort, medieval charm and twentieth-century plumbing – a fine combination. It's the only hotel I know where one changes elevators to get from the ground floor to some rooms on the third floor. I stayed in a room that had a private chapel. There were art works in the corridors, old paintings and carved Madonnas, but they were securely fastened to the walls. Even in Rothenburg one has to be careful of certain guests who might be temped to take a souvenir along.

HEIDELBERG
Baden-Württemberg, West Germany

EW PEOPLE go to Heidelberg just to see the place. Most return there to find a personal memory, a touch of nostalgia, or a better past. Some studied in Heidelberg long ago, and some fell in love there. Or perhaps they know of it from a book or song, a play or poem. Each person feels he's known Heidelberg long before he actually arrives. Such an image is an advantage but does have its drawbacks. Romantics in search of Old Heidelberg may possibly find it if they arrive on a warm summer evening when the air is full of scents and sounds. Heidelberg's sunsets are said to be the most beautiful in Germany (where people are aware of such things). The lights seem to rise from the Neckar and the Rhine and the air is soft, almost caressing. The illuminated Castle and the Old Bridge are reflected in the river. In 1797, long before son et lumière was invented, Goethe wrote about his impressions of the Old Bridge, the roofs and the steeples in his diary. To have been mentioned by Goethe means more in Germany than Michelin's three-star accolade does in France. Ever since then Heidelberg has been Germany's unofficial super dream town.

However, if you make the mistake of visiting Heidelberg during the long tourist season you may not find much time for admiration and contemplation. You will be elbowed aside by sightseeing maniacs or colour film fans, stuck in streets jammed with cars, and unable to get a table at a restaurant. Inevitably you'll see such unromantic signs as 'Sale of Antik [sic] Furniture', 'Shepherd's Lounge', 'Old Timer Club', 'Sex Messe', and 'Barbier [sic] Shop'. Old inns have become steak houses and former hangouts are discothèques. Time, the greatest mover of all, has not bypassed Heidelberg, and time now endangers its romantic charm, which is still there but getting harder to find. The old arcades of the Bismarckplatz have disappeared to make room for a department store. Heidelberg is, after all, part of the German economic miracle. A German friend who visited after an absence of fifteen years told me he hardly recognized the place. Beautiful façades are smeared with the political slogans of the Communist minority among Heidelberg's thirty thousand students. Some pseudo-student princes of yesterday escape into the closed world of their corporations, but most students work hard in Heidelberg, nor can they afford to live in the Old Town. Some go to nearby villages such as Handschuhsheim (now part of Heidelberg) for the charm and tranquillity of enjoying warm *Zwiebelkuchen* (onion cake) and young wine in a tavern.

Heidelberg's formidable remaining fortifications.

Go to Heidelberg on a quiet Sunday morning in spring when the students and soldiers are still asleep (Heidelberg is the headquarters of the US Army in Europe) and you will have the town to yourself. There are different ways of coming back to Heidelberg, and all are good. Some walk up the Philosophenweg (Philosophers' Way) to look down at the Old Town and the Castle of Yettenbuehl Hill, the trees on Heiligenberg, and the haze coming up from the Neckar. St Nepomuk looks down at the river, and on the Old Bridge the statues of Pallas Athena and Elector Carl Theodor greet the visitor. There are fine baroque houses in Corn Market as well as the Madonna and Child; the genuine 'Alt Heidelberg' area lies between Karl's Square and University Square, where the Old and the New Universities are located. The Augustin Monastery once stood where Luther in 1517 held his famous disputation.

This town became the birthplace and heart of German romanticism, not just a literary, artistic or musical movement but a way of life. At Hauptstrasse 151 (which is still there) two poets, Clemens Brentano and his brother-in-

Despite a great deal of modernization and foreign influence Heidelberg still exudes an old world charm.

law Achim von Arnim, published *Des Knaben Wunderhorn*, a collection of German folk songs that influenced the poet Joseph von Eichendorff and others, starting a new vogue of German nationalism. The brothers Boisserée collected paintings of long-forgotten German and Flemish masters that they had discovered in monasteries around Cologne, then under French occupation, and set up their collection in a fine palace on Karl's Square. Among their visitors was Goethe, then sixty-five, who came in 1814 and stayed two weeks. The collection is now part of the Pinakothek in Munich. Goethe himself returned the following year with Marianne von Willemer and walked around the castle meditating on his *East-West Divan*. His romantic days were over and he was now a strict classicist, but the Heidelberg movement grew and became part of Germany's national consciousness.

Heidelberg is much older than German romanticism, though the two have become synonymous. The earliest known inhabitants of the area were the Celts in the first century BC; the Heiligenberg (Saints' Mountain) overlooking the city was originally a Celtic settlement. The Celts were wiped out by

The Old Bridge, roofs and steeples which captured Goethe's interest.

the Teutons who in turn were driven back behind the Rhine by the Roman legions. They built their camp in the part of Heidelberg now known as Neuenheim, later settled on both sides of the Neckar, planted vineyards, and built a temple in honour of Mercury. The Romans were driven out around 260 AD by the Alemanni and for a while the area was dominated by rival German kingdoms. At this time woods still grew where the Old Town is now. Benedictine monks founded St Michael's Monastery on the Heiligenberg and St Stephen's farther below; both are now ruins. 'Heidelberch' was first mentioned in 1196 in a document of the Cistercian Monastery of Schönau. Later under Ludwig the Severe – so severe he had his own wife beheaded because he suspected her of flirting with one of his courtiers – Heidelberg became capital of the *Pfalz* (the Palatinate). Kurfürst Ludwig was one of the seven powerful princes who elected the emperor. It was one of his sons, Ruprecht, who in 1386 founded the University of Heidelberg, one of the oldest and most famous in Europe, modelled on the University of Paris, with a Rector at its head and four faculties (theology, law, medicine and free arts). It was a church institution, but only a hundred years later a married layman was admitted as a professor.

The intervening years were a time of religious crisis. Ruprecht II drove out the Jews and extended the city walls. His son Ruprecht III was elected German emperor and built the Holy Ghost Church. In Prague Jan Huss, Rector of the University and a disciple of the English heretic Wycliffe, attacked the Catholic hierarchy and rejected the dogma of transubstantiation. At the Council of Constance Ruprecht's son Ludwig III, chief judicial officer of the Holy Roman Empire, personally sentenced Huss to be burned at the stake.

The Schism ended in 1418 but in Heidelberg the religious problems continued. Martin Luther was received with enthusiasm at the University, and early in 1546 Lutheran services were held at the Holy Ghost Church. Under Elector Ottheinrich (Otto Henry), perhaps the most admired ruler of the Palatinate, Lutheranism was officially introduced. Ottheinrich built the beautiful Renaissance wing of the castle that is named after him and founded the famous Palatinate Library. He died childless in 1559 and was succeeded by Friedrich III, who renounced Lutheranism and accepted the more ascetic Calvinism. He ordered the Heidelberg Catechism to be drawn up, had many religious works of art burned, and turned the churches into sober structures, making Heidelberg a sort of German Geneva. Many Huguenot refugees came, among them the rich cloth merchant Charles Bélier who built the Hans zum Ritter (now a 'Romantik Hotel') and became mayor of Heidelberg.

When the defenestration in Prague started the terrible Thirty Years' War, the German princes elected Ferdinand of Habsburg as Catholic Emperor, but in Bohemia the Protestant nobles rejected Ferdinand and elected Kurfürst Friedrich V of the Palatinate as King of Bohemia. Friedrich and his ambitious wife Elizabeth, an English princess, accepted the challenge and went to Prague. It was said that Elizabeth 'would rather eat sauerkraut with a king than roast meat with an elector'. Alas, poor Friedrich was king only for one winter; in the spring, his Protestant forces were defeated by General Tilly at the White Mountain near Prague. The 'Winter King' fled to Brandenburg with his wife and child, and in Prague twenty-seven Protestant noblemen were executed. In 1622 Tilly captured Heidelberg after a two-month siege. His soldiers looted the town and Tilly ordered the Palatine Library to be removed from the gallery of the Holy Ghost Church and presented it to the pope in Rome. Many of the books and manuscripts are still at the Vatican.

But the worst was yet to come. On 2 March 1689, during the Palatinate Succession War, the French troops occupying the town executed orders of Louis XIV and looted the castle, mined it and blew up the front of the Fat Tower. The *Rathaus* went up in flames while General Mélac looked on with benign indifference. Fortunately his second-in-command, Lieutenant General Tessé, disagreed with the order and told the citizens 'to build small fires in their homes and make as much smoke as possible'. Only thirty-four

Heidelberg

houses burned down. But the war continued; in 1693 Mélac was back in Heidelberg and this time the French did a thorough job. The Castle fortifications were destroyed and the city was levelled. (It may be a coincidence, but in villages near Heidelberg many dogs are still called 'Mélac'.) Only a few stone buildings survived, among them the Haus zum Ritter. The Sun King ordered a medal struck to commemorate the annihilation: it shows the words HEIDELBERGA DELETA.

The destroyed Gothic town had had many half-timbered buildings, but the new town was rebuilt during the eighteenth century in stone. In 1799, during the French Revolution, Heidelberg was again briefly occupied by the French. In 1803 the former capital of the Palatinate became part of Baden and was ruled from Karlsruhe, an upstart town founded as late as 1715. But Grand Duke Karl Friedrich of Baden gave new financial support to the troubled Heidelberg University, renamed Ruperto Carola. In 1810 Count Charles François de Graimberg, a rich enthusiast and mediocre painter, came to Heidelberg and fell in love with it, as so many before and after him. His own paintings and drawings of the badly ruined castle started a campaign all over Germany and eventually Heidelberg Castle became a public monument, one of the world's most prominent and probably most expensive ruins. It is still kept in impeccable condition, exactly as it looked when the French had finished with it. It was already a special attraction in 1815, when Heidelberg became headquarters of the so-called Holy Alliance (which was neither holy nor a real alliance) and the Emperor of Austria came for a visit. In His Majesty's honour the Castle was beautifully illuminated.

Heidelberg continued to play an important role in German politics. In 1848 liberal and radical members of south German parliaments gathered there and called for a German national assembly that would ultimately create a unified Germany. Unification was still a long way off, and over 100,000 'Forty-Eighters', many from Baden, went to America as political *emigrés*. Tired of wars and revolutions, of being occupied and burned down, Heidelberg settled back and escaped into the never-never romanticism of 'Alt Heidelberg'. Those were the days – and the nights. The myth of beer drinking, fencing, songs and duels captured the imagination of people in Germany and abroad. Viktor von Scheffel wrote 'Alt Heidelberg, du feine', the song that became synonymous with the city, and his *Gaudeamus* cycle is still popular. In 1899 Wilhelm Meyer-Förster (from northern Germany, not from Heidelberg) wrote his story *Karl Heinrich* about the prince who comes to Heidelberg as a student, falls in love with a local girl and naturally must give her up, because he is a prince. Later Meyer-Förster wrote his sentimental play *Alt Heidelberg*, which became a great success. A young man named Sigmund Romberg saw it in Vienna, was impressed, and later wrote the operetta *The Student Prince*. It was a smash hit on Broadway in 1924, nine touring companies performed it all over America, and Heidelberg became a legend in the United States.

Heidelberg was a Social Democratic bastion during the Weimar Republic, but in 1933 over forty-one per cent voted for the National Socialist Party. During the Third Reich academic freedom was non-existent at the University, and one professor even taught 'Aryan physics', whatever that was.

Heidelberg by night, showing the castle and the Karl-Theodor bridge over the River Neckar.

94

LEFT *View of Heidelberg from the* Philosophenweg *(Philosopher's Walk)*.

RIGHT *Heidelberg Castle is a magnificent red sandstone structure, begun in the thirteenth century but not completed until the Renaissance.*

During the final days of the Second World War, the 44th US Infantry Division under Major General William Beiderlinden moved against Heidelberg. The general's grandfather had been a Forty-Eighter from Germany; he himself had read Meyer-Förster's *Alt Heidelberg* in school. After some negotiations, Heidelberg surrendered and the Americans moved in. The bridges had been destroyed by the retreating Germans, but the city was saved; no bomb fell, no shot was fired. Again, the myth had been stronger than reality. 'No history of Heidelberg should overlook the influence of Meyer-Förster,' General Beiderlinden wrote later.

The castle remains the great tourist attraction, with its confusing variety of styles, resulting from the changes or additions of almost every Palatine ruler. Its main attraction is the 'giant barrel', holding exactly 46,732 gallons of wine, which the rulers liked to have well filled. Elector Carl Philipp had brought to Heidelberg a short man named Clemens from the South Tyrol and made him cellarmaster. Any time Clemens was asked whether he wanted more wine he would say '*Perchè no?*' (why not?), and he became immortal as 'the dwarf Perkeo'. He is said to have died after drinking a litre of water.

Heidelberg University, re-opened in 1946, is again one of the world's great institutions of academic freedom; some think perhaps *too* much freedom. One of the publishers of the new *Rhein-Neckar-Zeitung* was Theodor Heuss, who became President of the Federal Republic. The students' gaol, used until 1914, is now a tourist attraction and open for inspection. Apparently 'Alt Heidelberg' will never die – which may be just as well.

PARMA
Emilia, Italy

EVEN IN ITALY, paradise of uninhibited individualists, the *Parmigiani*, the citizens of Parma, are considered somewhat *bizzarro*. In Italy that's a compliment, of course, and Parma is much respected. Freedom has a particular meaning to the *Parmigiani*, who played an important role during the *Risorgimento*, and in this century Parma was probably the last Italian city to accept Mussolini, with the greatest reluctance.

Parma gave the Italians their greatest, best-loved composer. Giuseppe Verdi was born in the tiny village of Le Roncole, not far from Parma, in 1813 when the Duchy of Parma still belonged to Napoleon's empire. After the Congress of Vienna, Metternich installed the Habsburg Archduchess Marie-Louise as 'puppet ruler' of the Duchy. But Marie-Louise, the wife and later the widow of Napoleon, often showed her independence, which displeased Metternich in Vienna. When Verdi dedicated to her the score of his second opera, *I Lombardi*, he acted out of gratitude, and even the Italian patriots didn't mind. Maria-Luigia, as they called her in Parma, did much for the arts as well. She founded the Convitto Maria-Luigia, sometimes known as 'the Italian equivalent of Eton', made the ancient Palatine Library at the Palazzo della Pilotta one of the finest on earth, and supported the printing press of G. B. Bodoni, who gave his name to a typeface which is still in use. Her court orchestra was famous in Italy, but then the Habsburgs were always music-minded. In 1831 (Verdi was not yet eighteen) the Duke of Reichstadt ('L'Aiglon'), son of Napoleon and Marie-Louise, was proclaimed 'Napoleon II, King of Italy' in the Duchy of Modena, near Parma. Marie-Louise was kept 'prisoner' by the Carbonari, the revolutionaries in Parma, but she was soon permitted to escape to Piacenza, then still under Austrian control. The Duke of Reichstadt died of tuberculosis in Vienna at the age of twenty-one, eighteen months after the revolt, and was buried there. Marie-Louise was buried next to him in 1847.

When Verdi made his first trip to Milan, then part of a 'foreign' state, he carried a passport issued by Parma's Ministry of the Interior, describing his nose as 'aquiline', his complexion as 'pale', and his special peculiarities as 'pock marks'. In 1855, Verdi wanted to go to France and England. Parma had no treaties with these countries, and he needed a new passport and visas. There was much red tape involved, and some people advised Verdi to become a citizen of another state. He was already world-famous and every country would have been happy to have him. But Verdi wrote to his lawyer

Parma Cathedral photographed from the west; on the right, the Baptistery, one of the finest in Italy.

Parma

LEFT *The nave of Parma Cathedral is painted with frescoes by fifteenth- and sixteenth-century artists.*

Details of the excellent carved stonework on the exterior of the Baptistery.

in Busseto near Parma: 'I wish to remain what I am, a peasant from Le Roncole.' He always called himself 'a peasant from Parma', even after his moving hymn *Va, Pensiero*, sung by the chorus of the Israelites in his opera *Nabucco*, became the unofficial anthem of the *Risorgimento*, and Italian patriots scrawled VIVA VERDI on walls in defiance of the Austrian soldiers. VERDI was an acronym for '*Vittorio Emanuele Re d'Italia*'. To the Italians, Verdi is a great musician *and* a great patriot.

Italy is the birthplace of opera, and nowhere in Italy is opera as ardently loved and violently discussed as in Parma – not even around La Scala in Milan. Parma's Teatro Regio, built during the reign of Maria-Luigia, is certainly the world's most enthusiastic opera house. Intimate and elegant, with red plush and gold-leaf, and a capacity of only 1300 people, it isn't a

'big' house but has seen the downfall of many famous stars since it was opened in 1829 with Bellini's *Zaira*. The *Parmigiani* are said to know and care more about opera than other Italians. Even the poor queue up for hours to get a seat in the gallery. In Parma practically everyone is opera-crazy. Even celebrated singers have trembled when they appeared at the Teatro Regio. The emotionally supercharged local aficionados either cheer enthusiastically or whistle angrily. It is a devastating sort of whistling, *il fischio*. A local story tells of a famous tenor who arrived at the railroad station and was warmly welcomed by two porters. They took his luggage and told him they could hardly wait to hear him in *Aida* the following night. But the poor tenor was nervous and in the difficult 'Celeste Aida' aria at the beginning he cracked the final B-flat. The angry *Parmigiani* started *il fischio*. The story doesn't tell how Radames got through the four acts before he mercifully dies, but when the tenor left Parma he had to carry his own luggage. No porter at the station would help him. People who know the Teatro Regio audiences are convinced the story is true. Once the American baritone Cornell MacNeil got so angry by *il fischio* that he shouted at the gallery, '*Cretini!*' Some people rather liked that. It proved that *il Americano* took Parma seriously, as one should.

The Teatro Regio was not the earliest opera house in Parma. In 1618 Ranuccio Farnese commissioned the famous Aleotti of Argenta to build a theatre for 3000 people where fine performances of the works of Monteverdi were later given. There were other theatres; under the Bourbons the best composers and singers of the day would appear in Parma. Between 1843

The Biblioteca Palatina owes its fine and extensive collection in part to the interest of Napoleon's widow, Marie-Louise; it is primarily important for the original editions and type of Bodoni.

and 1951 (when Verdi's death in 1901 was commemorated), 1382 performances of almost all Verdi operas were given in Parma. The composer had been very fond of the Teatro Regio ever since he had supervised a *Nabucco* production there in 1843 with Giuseppina Strepponi. He later fell in love with Giuseppina, and they lived together for years until he married her in 1859. There had been much gossip and scandal about Giuseppina in Busseto and Parma at the time, but now the *Parmigiani* claim the great love affair started in Parma, though they know it isn't true. In 1872 Verdi supervised a production of *Aida* in Parma, this time with Teresa Stolz in the title role, and again there was gossip.

Gossip and music go well together in Parma. Cleofonte Campanini, born in Parma in 1860, studied and made his debut there, and later became one of the great opera conductors of this century. In 1914 he organized the famous contest in Parma at which Beniamino Gigli was discovered. 'We found *the* tenor,' wrote Alessandro Bonci in his report. Bonci himself was a famous tenor who had made his debut in Parma. Arturo Toscanini was born in 1867 in a poor street in the old town, studied at the Conservatory, and began his career as a cellist in the orchestra of the Teatro Regio. The noted Italian composer Ildebrando Pizzetti was born in Parma in 1880 and studied there. The great Renata Tebaldi, though born in Pesaro, studied in Parma with Carmen Melis which, as they say in Parma, makes her almost a *Parmigiana*.

Parma is located in the region of Emilia, along the old Roman road known as Via Emilia (and the more recent *autostrada del sole*). The Via Emilia cuts from the Po at Piacenza to Rimini on the Adriatic. In wintertime Parma is often shrouded by the dense fogs of the Po Valley, and the old houses and churches disappear in a ghostly mist. Farmers walk by, wearing their long cloaks thrown across their shoulders, looking like the conspirators in Verdi's *Un Ballo di Maschera*. The people of Parma claim they are quite different from the people in Reggio nell' Emilia, Bologna and Ravenna. They speak their own dialect and use many French words. In Parma *vino* becomes *vin*, a bottle cork *(turacciolo)* is a *bouchon*, and a *carciofo* (artichoke) is *un artichaut*. The old French habits are hard to get rid of. All Italians like pretty women, but in Parma's Piazza Garibaldi girl-watching is the men's favourite pastime. The girls, famous for their grace and elegance, don't seem to mind. The *Parmigiani* also like old paintings, especially those made by their own masters, Correggio and Parmegianino. Correggio's fresco of the Assumption at Parma's twelfth-century Romanesque cathedral is a great masterpiece of Renaissance art.

Parma has many beautiful buildings, such as the churches of Madonna della Steccata and of San Giovanni Evangelista, the *centro episcopale* and the *battistero*. The National Museum of Former Ages holds splendid Etruscan and Roman antiquities. Some of Italy's finest art collections are at the strange-looking Palazzo della Pilotta, a large and unfinished Spanish-style structure of brick. The noble dynasty of the Farnese lived there for 148 years until the family died out. Inside is the Teatro Farnese, decorated with mythological and equestrian statues. Three hundred years ago baroque spectacles were produced on the vast stage, and hydraulic machinery was used to show terrific battles between sea monsters.

Parma

One can't help liking the *Parmigiani*. Whatever they do, they do with great gusto. On Sundays the women, wearing black shawls, are crowded inside the churches, while the men stand outside, talking interminably, as is expected of Italian Communists. If that reminds you of the little world of Don Camillo, it is no accident. Alberto Guareschi was a *Parmigiano*. Parma is not as 'radical' as Reggio nell' Emilia 'where even the dogs wear party membership tags', but 'even our capitalists are Communists', according to several witnesses. The old men wear black felt hats like the one in pictures of Verdi as an old man. In Le Roncole, now called 'Roncole Verdi', the Guareschi family runs a very good restaurant, featuring *cannelloni Rigoletto*.

Food means almost as much as music to the people of Parma, who invented one of the world's most famous cheeses. In Parma, you don't ask simply for *Parmigiano* or, God forbid, for Parmesan, showing your abysmal ignorance. (In Bordeaux, you certainly wouldn't ask for 'wine'.) You must be specific. Ask for a *stravecchio* that has been maturing for at least two years in a dim *maggazzino di formaggio*, a special warehouse built for that purpose. In the case of other internationally famous specialities, the finest qualities are often exported, but not in Parma, where the local people talk dreamily about 'vintages' of *Parmigiano*, exactly as the people in wine regions talk about their wines. To test Parmesan and show that you know it, bite into a piece before you buy it to see whether it has the right crunch. The *Parmigiani* keep the best varieties for themselves, and the rest of Italy and the outside world will have to take what's left. A bowl of grated *Parmigiani* stands ready on every Italian table: no Italian spends a day without eating *past'asciutta* at least once, and the pasta is always served with *Parmigiano*.

The people of Parma claim they eat better than most other Italians, and they claim it even in the company of people from Bologna who are convinced that their cooking is best. The *Parmigiani* only smile at such boasts; discussing food is as risky there as discussing opera. They know, of course, that their *culatello* is the finest smoked ham in Italy. They would never ask for *jambon de Parme* or even for San Daniele; that's for the capitalists who don't know better. *Culatello* is tender and delicate, cut in almost transparent slices. Gabriele d'Annunzio, the eccentric poet, once compared its taste to the breasts of a beautiful woman, and no one in Parma thought that was *bizzarro*. It is said that the finest *culatello* comes from the village of Zibello; Verdi loved it. And they are proud of their salami from Felino; *porcino nero* ('the little black pig') from Borgotaro, which isn't pig at all but a luscious mushroom; and they love the large sweet tomatoes from Sala Baganza. Local housewives make small *tortelli* or smaller *tortellini di erbette parmigiana*, tiny pasta packages filled with ricotta cheese, eggs, spinach, butter and, naturally, *grana*, as the local connoisseurs call their crisp, crunchy Parmesan cheese. Yes, one eats very well in and around Parma.

When the *Parmigiani* aren't eating or listening to opera they are probably sitting in a café talking and looking at their beautiful women. What the Regio is to opera-lovers, the Café Bizzi on Via Cavour is to women-watchers. The opera stage is replaced by *passeggio*, the sidewalk promenade. Everyone is astonishingly well-dressed. The men like good suits and wear them proudly, with silver watch chains over their waistcoats and Borsalino hats;

This overall view of Parma shows the harmonious blend of its diverse architecture.

they are the best-dressed Communists in the world, and that includes the
Kremlin. The women often look like duchesses, and perhaps they are. Some
seem to have stepped out of a Correggio or Parmigianino, *naturale*. The
pretty women are pointed out as a great sight, almost like those in a
Correggio. On Wednesdays and Saturdays, however, they are not visible.
On these days the piazza is taken over by the *contadini*, farmers who come
from the countryside to buy and sell. Many look and talk like operatic
characters, with sonorous baritone voices. *Naturale* – this is Verdi country.

CREMONA
Lombardy, Italy

CREMONA IS UNIQUE. Its Piazza Domenico (now called Piazza Roma) was at one time the home of the greatest violin-makers the world has known. Around the turn of the eighteenth century Antonio Stradivari, the most celebrated master of all, lived at Number Five with his sons Francesco and Omobono Felice. A sidestreet led to the parish of San Faustino and the patrician house of the Amati family. The Amatis had lived in Cremona since 1007. Andrea Amati, the first violin-making member of the family, was most probably the genius who was primarily responsible for creating the violin. The oldest surviving instruments were made by him around 1550. These early violins were already so well-made that even Stradivari didn't try to improve the basic design. As a work of art the violin is a phenomenon: it was born, as we know it today, a marvel of mathematics, physics, chemistry and acoustics. It remains a miracle, emerging in perfect finished form. No one has ever been able to explain this mystery satisfactorily.

Very close to the house of Stradivari was the parish of San Matteo, where Andrea Guarneri's modest house was situated. The noble though somewhat impoverished Guarneri family has been traced back to 1209 in Cremona. Andrea Guarneri, born in 1626, was the first of the family's five violin-makers. He had two sons, Pietro Giovanni (later known as 'Pietro of Mantua') and Giuseppe Giovanni ('Joseph filius Andreae'). Giuseppe's son, the great Giuseppe Guarneri del Gesù, became the family's most illustrious member, and the most mysterious. His life and work are surrounded by legends and mysteries which modern experts have not completely solved. He lived in the parish of San Prospero, less than five minutes from Stradivari's house. He made only violins while most of the other masters also made violas and cellos. The finest Guarneri del Gesù violins are as valuable now as the great Stradivari instruments and may one day be worth more since there are not many of them; they are famous for tonal beauty and sonorous power.

Nearby was the house of Carlo Bergonzi, for centuries believed to be the 'favourite pupil of Stradivari'. We know better today. But Bergonzi's instruments – he made less than a hundred – are beautiful and valuable. Close to Bergonzi's home was the house of Francesco Ruggieri. He, like Andrea Guarneri and Antonio Stradivari, were pupils of Nicolò Amati, greatest of the Amatis and the finest teacher in Cremona. Thus the circle is closed.

Most of the world's finest string instruments – violins, violas, cellos – have

Il Torrazzo, a Gothic campanile dating from 1250, is the highest in Italy.

A general view showing the Palazzo Comunale, behind which is the cathedral and the famous Torazzo.

come from this relatively small section of Cremona. And most of them were made within two hundred years. That's another mystery no one can explain. No similar phenomenon exists in any of the other arts. No single place can claim to have exclusively produced, within a relatively short time, the finest paintings, the greatest sculptures, or the best wood carvings. (A violin includes all three.) There were fine violin-makers elsewhere, such as Gasparo da Salò, one of the earliest creators and pioneers, who came from nearby Brescia. Domenico Montagnana, Santo Seraphin and Matteo Gofriller were Venetian masters. There was Jacob Stainer in Absam, in the Tyrol (once as famous as Stradivari), Giovanni Baptista Guadagnini in Parma, the Gagliano family in Naples, the Grancino family and Carlo Ferdinando Landolfi in Milan. But no town comes close to Cremona in sheer concentration of talent. The monopoly of the Cremonese masters was never challenged.

Cremona's visible history goes as far back as the decades after 1000 AD when the beautiful Romanesque and later Gothic buildings were created to form the heart of the city. The Duomo, with its powerful Lombard-Romanesque façade, was not only the cathedral but the centre of public life in Cremona. (It is located in the heart of the former 'violin district'.) Cremona was then free but eventually lost its independence to Milan in 1344. Ninety years later, the Duchy of Milan, with Cremona, became part of Spain. During the Renaissance, Cremona was the home of a modest school of painting. In the early sixteenth century, when Andrea Amati was born (the exact date is unknown), Cremona had lost its political significance and become a sleepy provincial town on the left bank of the River Po. There were only the noble squares and beautiful *palazzi*, and the four hundred foot-high *Torrazzo*, Italy's highest bell tower.

Even the proud Cremonese wouldn't claim that their town might compare with Florence, Venice, Rome or half a dozen other Italian cities. But there was an inherited sense of beauty and a peaceful feeling of harmony about the town and countryside. That may partly explain why nearly all important string instruments were created there: the climate is warm and dry; the people know the value of patience. Stradivari would hang up his freshly varnished instruments to dry slowly on the *seccadour*, the flat terrace on the roof of his house. During the warm season he liked to work up there in the bright light and fresh air.

Much nonsense has been written about the varnish, the most 'mysterious' component of the violin that gives a well-built instrument its distinctive timbre. The composition of the Cremonese varnish is no secret, and every amateur maker knows it: gums soluble in oil with colouring ingredients added. But no one has come up with as fine a varnish as was once made in Cremona. The former resins and dyestuffs used by the old makers are no longer available in our age of synthetics. Marco Polo had brought to Venice from the Orient a substance known as 'dragon's blood', derived from the fruit of the Malayan palm tree. Stradivari's supplies often came from nearby Venice, and perhaps this exotic material was one of his ingredients.

But above all, methods have changed. The Cremonese makers wouldn't violate the laws of nature by hanging their instruments to dry in plain, hot sunshine. They were not in a hurry. In one of his two handwritten letters

known to exist, Stradivari writes, 'I beg you will forgive the delay concerning the violin, caused by the varnishing of the large cracks, so the sun may not re-open them.' Oil varnish dries slowly even in the warm climate of Cremona. Every detail of Stradivari's greatest instruments was executed with a sense of perfection, but it is the varnish that is most admired.

People visiting Cremona today also need patience and empathy. When I first came there in 1948, hoping to find an evocation of the town's great past, there was little. The houses of the great violin-makers had disappeared, and so had their works. Not a single great Cremonese violin was left in the place where they had been created. The great makers had been famous in France, Spain, Austria and England long before they were appreciated in their hometown. When the French armies passed through Cremona in 1795, the commanding general wanted to buy an Amati or a Stradivari. He was told there were none for sale.

I tried to talk to some citizens about the great men who made Cremona famous, but they stared at me uncomprehendingly. A travel folder said that Cremona was noteworthy 'chiefly for its specialities, such as butter and cheeses, mustards and sausages, marmalade and *torrone*', the last being a candy made of nuts, fruit, honey and sugar. I met Mario Stradivari, sixth-generation descendant of the great Antonio, an imposing Renaissance figure with wit and a sense of irony. Mario was a noted criminal lawyer who devastated his foes with sarcastic remarks. In 1937, an exposition of Stradivari

La Rocca Viscontea – Cremona's medieval fortress.

violins was held in Cremona commemorating the maker's two hundredth anniversary, but Mario wasn't invited. He had never seen a genuine Stradivari violin. His father Libero, also a famous lawyer, a follower of Garibaldi, and a close friend of Puccini, had left his son Mario a signed photograph of Giuseppe Verdi, but nothing that had once belonged to their great ancestor.

Cremona now has a Stradivari violin, just one, at the Municipal Museum in Palazzo Communale where a few Stradivari relics are exhibited. Made in 1715, the violin was once played by the great Joseph Joachim, and is now called 'Il Cremonese'. A small sidestreet has been named Via Stradivari, leading off Piazza Roma where Stradivari's house once stood. After the house had been sold by his heirs, a tailor's shop appeared and then a café with a pool-room. *Sic transit....* The house was later torn down and a large office building with a pretentious marble façade put up. A marble panel above a window bears an Italian inscription, reading: 'Here stood the house where Antonio Stradivari brought the violin to admirable perfection and left to his Cremona an imperishable name as a master of his craft.'

Anyone trying to visit the grave of Stradivari meets with embarrassed silence: there is no grave. The greatest violin-maker, Stradivari, and the greatest musical genius, Mozart, have no graves. Mozart was dumped into an unmarked mass grave at Vienna's St Marx Cemetery (in wintertime, which includes the dates of Mozart's birth and death, the cemetery is closed). Stradivari, whose birthdate remains unknown, was buried on 19 December 1737 in the family grave at the Chapel of the Rosary, in the Church of San Domenico. There he remained for 132 years. In 1869, when there was no money to repair and restore the church, it was decided to pull it down, and to use the site more 'profitably'. A firm from Milan was brought in for the job, and an eyewitness, Alfonso Mandelli, then a young man, was there when the tomb of Stradivari was wrecked. He heard someone say, 'There is such a confusion of bones that it seems useless to make any further search....' During the following days he watched men with baskets clear the tomb of all human bones. 'I learnt afterwards that the men interred the bones outside the city.' No other grave has been found, and it is now assumed that the workers simply walked to the bank of the Po, just a few minutes away, and threw the bones into the river.

For many years a simple round stone with the name STRADIVARI stood in a small park near the former site of the San Domenico Church. Mario Stradivari (who also happened to be a noted amateur composer) wrote the lyrics and tune for a song which goes: 'They say that the old Stradivari comes at night into the park to look at his monument but alas! all he finds are two mongrels who use the round stone for their needs.' Perhaps it was the bitter song that made the city fathers do something. At any rate, they had the old tombstone (which had been preserved) placed in the ground between flower beds on the former site of the grave. It says 'Sepolcro di Antoni Stradivari a. Svoi Eredi, Anno 1729'. That was the year Stradivari, already an old man, bought the family grave. There is also a small cross with the initials A.S., the circled monogram that Stradivari put on all his labels.

The people of Cremona had shown a similar lack of comprehension much

earlier when they set up their Academy of the Animosi in 1560 to preserve
Cremona's cultural heritage. Membership was restricted to the city's aristocratic families, and Andrea Amati, whose violins were already famous, was
not invited to join. In 1607, the Academy performed a concert selection from
La Favola d'Orfeo, one of the earliest surviving operas. It was written by Claudio Monteverdi, who was born in Cremona in 1567. He soon left his native
town for nearby Mantua where the dynasty of the Gonzaga did for opera
and music what the Medici in Florence had earlier done for painting and
sculpture and what the Habsburgs in Vienna did for music. Monteverdi later
moved to Venice, where he managed the world's first commercial opera
house where everyone could buy a ticket for a performance. He is now
revered as a lonely Renaissance genius akin to Michelangelo. Eventually
an opera house was built in Cremona. But it wasn't called after their own
genius, Monteverdi. The Teatro Ponchielli in Cremona is named after the
nineteenth-century composer Amilcare Ponchielli, who had produced there
his first opera, *I Promessi Sposi*, which is now almost forgotten.

It doesn't matter though. The *genius loci* remains very strong in Cremona.
One feels it the moment one gets away from noisy automobile traffic in
jammed streets, from the colourful weekly cheese and *torrone* markets, into
the old part of the town around the great Duomo with the tall, beautiful bell

The Piazza del Comune (left) *is the centre of life in Cremona. It includes the Duomo (* right*), consecrated in 1107 but completed considerably later.*

tower. The piazza is covered with the large flat stones which were there when the Amatis, the Guarneris, and Stradivari and his sons walked in the dusk and talked shop. They were a friendly group – that much is known – and there was little jealousy amongst them. There would have been gossip: the erratic Guarneri del Gesù might be in trouble again. Many writers have embroidered fantasies about del Gesù's having been in prison 'after killing a man in a drunken brawl', and for a while some of his violins were known as 'prison fiddles'. However, none of these stories has stood up to modern research.

Cremona now has a *Scuola Internazionale di Luteria*, its own school of violin-making. It is a modest establishment, five minutes' walk and 300 years away from the former house of Antonio Stradivari. No pupil has as yet produced an instrument even faintly resembling the great masterpieces of the past. But the music of Claudio Monteverdi is now performed and admired all over the world. And the instruments of the Cremonese masters are heard wherever people love music. I'm even willing to bet that the greatness of Stradivari and Guarneri del Gesù will outlive the fame of Cremona's cheese and *torrone* candy.

VERONA
Veneto, Italy

VERONA IS A DREAM TOWN where dreams come alive and reality dissolves into a dream world. Day after day foreigners – mostly women, often from England and America – make the pilgrimage to the fine thirteenth-century building at 17–25 Via Cappello called Palazzo Capulet. It can hardly be seen from the street, which is often filled with people and noise, as are so many streets in Italy; but visitors seem to know exactly where to find the gate into the courtyard. There they stand, looking up at the flower-filled balcony where one of the great love stories of all time reached its unforgettable climax. Up on the balcony stood Juliet, pale and lovely, a flower herself. Below her, unseen, is Romeo who had swung across the wall of the garden on his rope ladder.

It matters little to visitors that the great lovers never existed, that their tragic love story never happened. They stand in the courtyard, wishing they were Juliet, loved by a Romeo. The poet's dream is stronger than mere reality. Owing to Bandello, and especially to Shakespeare, the dream has become almost history. There is no garden wall – perhaps there never was – but the pilgrims *know* that it stood there, long long ago. They don't mind the nearby souvenir shop with its faint aura of commercial exploitation. After another look they turn to continue their pilgrimage to the small convent where they visit *la tomba di Giulietta*. Both *la casa* and *la tomba* are mentioned in the unromantic *Guida Michelin*. They are there, *ergo* they exist. The women visitors often seem a little embarrassed, as though they know, deep down in their hearts, that this is an absurdly romantic visit.

But it is so beautiful, so dreamlike. The broken sarcophagus, the cloister, the Gothic windows, the dim light, the dark crypt, and the secret wedding are all there, exactly as in their dreams. Many visitors leave flowers. Some sign the guest book. Few notice the bust of Shakespeare standing somewhat aside. He doesn't really matter. He only created the dream.

My friends in Verona tell me that the women rarely visit the nearby Palazzo Montague where Romeo once 'lived'. Perhaps Romeo interests them only because he loved Juliet. But they always visit the balcony, and the grave of Juliet. Even the often cynical Veronese don't smile about the foreigners; they are practical and know that the *stranieri* bring money. Besides, who can tell, perhaps the whole thing *was* true. Near the small convent is a statue of Dante Alighieri who lived in Verona during his exile. What about Dante's Beatrice? Wasn't she real? And Dante's *Inferno*, don't

Fine old palaces surround the Piazza del Signori.

Verona

we all know that? So, since you happen to be in Verona, why don't you visit the Arena which, according to a local legend, inspired Dante to write about Inferno and Paradise?

To the world at large the Arena has become a catchword of mass tourism. On the international festival circuit, the Arena of Verona is a 'must'. To the Veronese, however, the Arena *is* Verona, embodying almost two thousand years of their town's violent history. A memorial stone commemorates the Roman gladiator Generosus who caught twenty-seven adversaries with his fighting net and then stabbed them with his lance. He was history, not fiction; he existed. So did two saints, Fermus and Rusticus, who died in this Arena, and the 160 heretics who were burned at the stake. The Arena's red marble arches have seen great weddings and splendid *corridas*, drunken Venetian courtesans, and people murdered for show while twenty thousand looked happily on.

Nowadays the Roman amphitheatre, built under Emperor Diocletian and seating over twenty-five thousand people, is often sold out during the spectacular open-air opera performances that have taken place every summer since 1913, except during the two world wars. In 1913, the Italians celebrated the centenary of their beloved Giuseppe Verdi. Three enterprising Veronese, the famous tenor Giovanni Zenatello (then a much admired Otello), the composer Ferruccio Cusinati, and the impresario Ottone Rovato suggested a project that would outshine all other Verdi memorials in Italy. They would produce *Aida* in the Arena. Many people said it couldn't be done. The Arena had served for tournaments, for fights between bulls and greyhounds, for carnivals and choreographic performances, but never for opera. Think of the acoustics. Would they be tolerable?

The doors of the Roman basilica of San Zeno Maggiore are adorned with magnificently carved bronze reliefs; below is a detail, third from the bottom, far right, of the open door.

LEFT *The Roman arena which reputedly inspired Dante's* Divine Comedy.

They made tests and the results were promising, but they knew that the real test would come only when the huge Arena was filled with tens of thousands of people. The first performance on 10 August 1913 remains a glorious event in the annals of Italian opera. Tullio Serafin conducted, Zenatello was Radames, and Zenatello's wife, the mezzo Maria Gray, sang the part of Amneris. The marble columns blended into the magnificent sets of Egyptian temples, but the unique feature in Verona was, and remains, the magic reciprocal effect between the audience and the amphitheatre. Long before the performance begins, people are caught by the powerful atmosphere of the dark sky, and dramatically lighted, phantom-like Roman walls. Finally the great moment arrives when all the listeners light their *mocoleti*, the tiny candles that turn the wide stone steps into fantastic circles of fire. This moment, not the tenor's high 'C', remains for many the great experience of '*Stagione lirica nell'Arena di Verona*'. It is a dreamlike vision which becomes more than the music, the staging and the singing. It exists nowhere else.

The Arena has always had its critics. Many prominent singers, afraid of its size, were afraid to appear there. Most who did called it a terrifying experience. Toscanini refused to conduct there. He wouldn't trust the acoustics nor the enormous distances—about a hundred feet between the conductor and the singers. Subtle *pianissimo* passages get lost in the enormous

FOLLOWING PAGES
LEFT *The magnificent yellow- and red-striped Palazzo della Ragione.*
RIGHT *Verona's Roman Amphitheatre; in the background, the Town Hall.*

amphitheatre. Close contact between stage and orchestra is often impossible. But few listeners remain immune to the magic of the place, which makes you forget that this is an opera performance and not life. One no longer thinks of the effort of getting there, finding a hotel room or a place to park the car. During the first season, *Aida* was performed eight times. It remains the most popular among the spectacular operas that are especially well suited to the Arena: *Mefistofele, Samson et Dalila, Carmen, Turandot.* But foremost is Verdi, with his *Aida, Trovatore, Rigoletto* and *La Forza del Destino.*

The Arena reflects the improbable history of Verona, which became a Roman colony in 89 BC. In 489 AD the Romans were thrown out by Theoderich, King of the East Goths who then made Verona his residence. He is known as the legendary Dietrich of Bern (meaning Verona, not the Swiss Berne). After the East Goths came the Langobards. At his palace in Verona, King Alboin forced his wife Rosamunde to drink wine out of the skull of her murdered father. That was unwise; four years later Rosamunde had her husband murdered. After Charlemagne defeated the Langobards, his son Pippin was installed as king in Verona. In the tenth century, the Magyars devastated Verona, and two hundred years later the Veronese League was founded against Emperor Frederick I Barbarossa. The League was followed by the regimes of the Signoria della Scala, the Visconti of

Several fine, old bridges span the Adige from Verona. The stone bridge with the graceful arches (left) *contrasts sharply with the fortress-like structures emphasized in this impressive aerial view of the Ponte Scaligero and the Castelvecchio* (below).

*Part of Ronda's charm is that it
seems inaccessible: it is built on the
edge of a rocky, 2000 foot-high table-
land (left) and is cleft by a 500-foot
wide gorge (below left).*

Milan, and the Carrara dynasty, and then came Verona's golden age when the town belonged to Venice, from 1405 to 1796. Then came the French, and after 1814 the Austrians who incorporated Verona into their network of fortifications – to no avail: in 1866 the Austrians had to cede Venice with Verona to the kingdom of Italy. In 1945 when the Americans liberated Verona, not one of the ten bridges across the Adige was intact. All of them had been blown up in the last days of the war, but all were speedily rebuilt.

Many people who come to Verona to hear a performance at the Arena believe they have 'no time' to look around. They miss a great deal. '*Verona, qui te viderit et non amarit protinus amore perditissimo,*' wrote Giovanni Cotta in his stilted, sixteenth-century Latin ('Verona, whoever sees you and doesn't love you at once is lost to the beauty of love'). A well-meant exaggeration. In the fourteenth century, Verona dominated nine cities in her part of the world. (The cities were entities in themselves, not part of 'Italy,' which didn't yet exist.) Some had wealth and power, such as Padua, Vicenza, Treviso, Brescia, Belluno, Feltre, Parma, Modena, Lucca. The Florentine chronicler Giovanni Villani accused 'the tyrants of Verona' of having an annual income of 700,000 guilders, 'more than any Christian ruler except the King of France'.

Verona, then called 'the marble city', was feared for its aggressive spirit. It was also famous for its palaces, bridges and squares. Piazza delle Erbe, once the forum, is today the centre of town site of the statue of the Madonna of Verona. Piazza del Signori is completely surrounded by fine old palaces, with Fra Giocondo's early-Renaissance Loggia del Consiglio: the twelfth-century Palazzo della Ragione with its yellow- and red-striped walls and magnificent staircase; Palazzo del Capitano; and the almost sinister Palazzo del Governo. Also in the Piazza is Zannoni's monument to Dante. Piazza Sta Anastasia has the marble statue of Paolo Caliari, better known as Paolo Veronese. Castelvecchio (now the Museo Civici), the fourteenth-century fortress of the Scaligeri, stands near the towers of the old stone bridge, Ponte Scaligero, across the Adige. The Ghibelline dynasty of the Scaligeri or Scaliger remains a favourite and controversial subject for Italian and German historians. They were statesmen, soldiers, patrons of the arts, and always dictators. Much of Verona's beauty was created under their regime, from 1260 to 1387. Cangrande, the greatest of them, attracted Dante and Giotto to his court.

The greatness of old Verona can be seen in the fabulous Museum of Art in the Castelvecchio on Corso Cavour. Here are a Romanesque dome with a Gothic nave (some German experts speak of 'a Gothic dome with a Romanesque façade'), an altar-painting by Titian, and a fine Romanesque cloister. Another sight among Verona's fifty-odd churches is San Fermo Maggiore, a Gothic church above a Romanesque crypt with fine frescoes and tombs. San Giorgio in Braida has paintings by Tintoretto, Caroto and Paolo Veronese. This last is notable as Paolo, born in Verona in 1528, spent much of his life and did most of his work in Venice.

Verona is a town of many faces and much hidden beauty. From the ruins of the Roman Theatre, where Shakespeare is performed in summer, one can see the river that seems to embrace the town in a giant 's'. The Giardino

Verona

Giusti is known for the majestic beauty of its cypresses. The mystical heart of Verona, however, is in the Roman basilica of San Zeno Maggiore, which contains Mantegna's triptych on the high altar and a marble statue of the African bishop who performed many miracles, Verona's patron saint. He is smiling, as are many Veronese much of the time. He is surrounded by magnificent reliefs depicting the stories of the Old and New Testaments for the benefit of those who never learned to read, of whom there were many in this overpopulated, impoverished district. Here they could also 'read' the story of Verona, of Nibelungs and German emperors, and of the fights of the free Commune. The bell tower was built in 1095. During the carnival, the bishop with the smiling chocolate face and the great ruler Cangrande again become symbols of Verona, joined by Papà del Gnocco, the robust Carnival King.

Those who love noise and movement find it in the market stalls and parasols of the Piazza delle Erbe (they remain there overnight) or in the small sidestreets and piazzettas of the Via Mazzini which reveal a confusing variety of balconies, windows, laundry, flowers, pigeons and, always, people. Or they can try the Piazza Bra, in itself encompassing two thousand years of history: the Arena, the trecento palace of the Visconti, the seicento of Gran Guardia and the settecento of the Teatre Filarmonico. Everybody who is anybody in Verona wants to be seen promenading before dinner. At old *trattorias* the local people sit at long wooden tables, polished like mirrors after decades of use. The best of them, called '12 Apostoli', is one of the best eating-places in the region.

Verona remains a town with many meanings. Until 1914 it was known as a 'fortress', because the Habsburgs had made it a cornerstone of their allegedly impregnable fortifications, which also included Peschiera, Mantua and Legnago. For many tourists it is just a place where they have to change trains. In the early afternoon fast trains from Athens, Copenhagen, Munich and Milan met there, almost at the same time, and for a while the last two porters were very busy. Today many motorists who have been to Naples or Venice probably don't bother to stop at Verona. Music lovers go there for a performance at the Arena, and many visit the annual *Fiera dell'Agricoltura e Zootecnica*; last year there were almost 4000 exhibitors and over 650,000 visitors. They even have a special 'salon' for tractors. But for those who love Italy and never tire of the gifted, cheerful, noisy Italians, Verona remains a normal, almost typical town, with its past and legends, songs and colours. More than a great many towns in Italy, Verona *is* Italy.

Colourful parasols characterize the market place of the Piazza delle Erbe which was once Verona's ancient forum.

RONDA
Andalusia, Spain

RONDA IS ONE OF THE LEAST KNOWN and most dramatic dream towns of Europe. Although geographically part of the Costa del Sol that stretches for almost 200 miles between Cabo de Gata and Tarifa, and which became the postwar miracle of international tourism, Ronda does not belong to the 'Spanish Riviera'. One of the oldest towns in Spain, Ronda is an hour away from Marbella, which boasts the supreme accolade of tourist prestige – a Hilton hotel; and even farther from Torremolinos, the super-chic resort with the super-fine beach. (Back in 1930 Marbella was a small sleepy town and Torremolinos had one small pension, frequented mostly by British eccentrics.)

Ronda is a different world, almost unspoiled, impressively located on a rocky plateau above the Tajo, a thousand-foot-deep chasm. 'Tajo' means 'cut' or 'cleft'. It was an ideal stronghold for any proud people who refused to surrender their independence.

Fiery Andalusian bandits at one time had their headquarters in Ronda. A Roman bridge leads to the not-so-old Mercadillo. And there the Moors rose for the last time against the Catholic monarchs, Ferdinand and Isabella. The Moorish *ciudad* (town) of Ronda stands isolated on the southern tip of the plateau in such a position that it cannot be attacked directly. Ferdinand found that out when he laid siege to Ronda in 1485. The only approach was by the Puerta de Almocabar at the western side (which later acquired a baroque gateway). Through this gate Ferdinand entered the city in a solemn victory procession that had its own mystical protocol. First, the standard of the Cross, a present from Pope Sixtus IV, was hoisted on a tower, and everybody knelt down, including the monarchs. Priests sang *Te Deum laudamus*, and only then was the banner of the sovereigns displayed, and the soldiers shouted 'Castile!' The official liberation of the Christian captives followed, and their chains were sent to Toledo, to be displayed in the Church of San Juan de los Reyes. Ferdinand and Isabella expected to be buried there, but changed their minds after the capture of Granada, the greatest treasure of Moorish Spain. This victory was the climax of the Reconquest, and the Catholic Monarchs 'wept with joy' as their flag was raised in 1492 on the tower of the Alhambra. Later they were buried in the royal chapel of the local cathedral. In Ronda one is reminded of them by the Church of the Holy Ghost which they founded. The purification and conversion of Ronda's chief mosque had already been completed.

A picturesque street in Ronda.

Ronda

Ronda is a way-station on the rocky road from Jerez de la Frontiera, hometown of sherry, so dear to the palates and hearts of Englishmen, to Málaga, another great wine town, the birthplace of Picasso. Ronda hasn't changed much since the eighteenth century when it was a romantic kingdom of smugglers. Some believe that Ronda may have been the scene of the third act of *Carmen*, with poor Don José doing guard duty for the smugglers and getting into a dangerous argument with Escamillo, the great *torero*.

Ronda also happens to be the place where the first *corrida* was held and brave men on foot dared fight the bulls. Until the late eighteenth century bulls were usually let loose in a public square, and aristocrats would fight them from horseback. Then the dangerous entertainment was forbidden by royal decree until a man from Ronda named Pedro Romero had the brilliant idea of fighting the bull on foot. The audacious Rondeño possibly saved Spain's great national sport. The first unmounted *corrida* took place in Ronda in 1786. Pedro Romero, then thirty-two, was the star. He remains an almost legendary figure in Ronda, said to have killed almost five thousand bulls during his long career; his last *corrida* was fought at the venerable age of eighty, at a benefit performance in Madrid. His house in Ronda's Alameda became almost a shrine, and other small houses in the district with a cross on the stone lintel once belonged to him. On 9 September there is a memorial *corrida*, with the participants dressed in historical costumes worn in the early nineteenth century. One sees them in the paintings of Goya. Pedro's son, Juan, lived to be 102 years old. Another member of the family, José Romero, retired in 1803, but at the age of seventy-three he made a dramatic comeback and killed four bulls. The Romeros were quite a family.

The Plaza de Toros was built in 1785, originally not as a bull ring but as a show place for the local equestrian society. At the Picadero de Maestranza the horses were shod. The Plaza de Toros is not only the oldest bull ring in Spain but also the largest. It is built of grey stone with two rows of Doric columns. Each of the two stories has a roof of its own. Another unique feature is the gate through which the bull is let out. In Ronda, the *toril* is just below the President's box, not opposite it, as elsewhere. Next to this box was one for the local church dignitaries. They would hold a service prior to the *corrida* at which all *toreros* were present. Then the dignitaries would retire to their box and watch the fighters they had just blessed as they were wounded or killed. Ronda is a hallowed place for aficionados. Ernest Hemingway would come there often, accompanied by a *torero* friend.

Next to bull fighting, Ronda also has a great tradition of smuggling, being ideally located on the road from Gibraltar to the Sierra Morena. The suburb of San Francisco was always popular with smugglers because goods passing through were exempt from city duties and could be conveniently 'processed'. Ronda is surrounded by the sierras of the Serranía of Ronda. ('Sierra' is the Spanish word for 'saw'.) Ronda's picturesque location has guaranteed its survival as a dream town and haven for artists and writers. The Alameda (public gardens), now called after José Antonio Primo de Rivera, is beautiful with roses, cassias, chestnuts and cedars, and offers a splendid view of the dramatic scenery. Passing the Plaza de Toros one

The first corrida *was held in Ronda; the Plaza de Toros, built in 1785, is the oldest and largest bull ring in Spain.*

sees the Teatro Espinel, called after Vicente Espinel who was born in Ronda in 1551. For a long time Espinel – Latin scholar, poet, soldier, priest – was erroneously known as the man who added the fifth string to the guitar when it had only four strings. He didn't improve the guitar, which now has six strings, but he composed music for the guitar, and he wrote *Adventures of Marcos Obregón* which became a classic. As so many people in Ronda, he lived to be very old. Perhaps it is the climate.

Farther on, the street leads toward the eighteenth-century Puente Nuevo, which spans the Tajo. The sides of the cliffs fall down almost vertically, and the piers of the bridge were constructed on foundations deep down in the bed of the Guadalevín river at the bottom of the gorge. The architect,

Ronda

José Martín de Aldehuela, fell from the bridge shortly before it was completed, and was killed. He may have lost his balance as he admired the view from the bridge which, some think, is worth the journey to Ronda. There was once a prison inside the bridge, reached by a stairway, that was later turned into a restaurant with barrel-vaulted ceilings and a stewpot hanging in the fireplace. The décor and the food were very Spanish. The cured ham, the famous *jambón serrano* from Montejaque, was carved from a leg that still had hoof and hair.

At the old Moorish town the streets are 'typical' and the African colour is strong. There are many ornaments on the doors. Plaza del Campillo, near the edge of the cliff, offers a fine view of the deep valley below. A footpath and a road lead to the power station and the mills in the river valley. Throughout the centuries, the river has had many uses: it provided steam for the early Arab baths and later became a pool for a queen; then it produced the water-power to grind corn in the mills, and finally to turn the turbines of the modern power station. Eventually the Guadalevín flows into the Guariaro river that joins the sea near Gibraltar. The view from below is almost as impressive as the view from the bridge.

The Convent of Santa Teresa was the last holdout of the French troops in 1812 after Marshal Nicolas Soult had withdrawn from Andalucía. The French were killed. Among the interesting African houses is the Mondragón Palace, built in the eighth century, that was later restored by the Catholic Monarchs. There is also the Casa del Gigante, with fine Arabic stucco work and framed mosaic *azulejo* on the walls. The Moslem atmosphere is strongly felt here. The neighbourhood is picturesque with Roman fragments, broken stones, and tiles of various periods. People who think they have no time to visit North Africa can get a taste of it in Ronda.

In Plaza de Trinidad Scholtz, formerly named after the Đuquesa de Parcent (who spent much of her own money on the restoration of the old town), is the Church of Santa María la Mayor; this was once the chief mosque of Ronda. One sees its history as one looks at the bell tower. Originally it was a minaret, with a square lower part and an octagonal upper part, almost like a belfry in Belgium. A double gallery was built into the façade, probably for spectators during bull fights who wanted a good view of the square. Inside are Gothic and Renaissance elements, an old *mihrab* with a horsehoe arch, fine Arabic stucco work and Oriental-styled Ionic volutes. This is of course primarily a church, but it would make a fine museum.

Nearby is the Alimar, once a minaret of a mosque, that was transformed into a church and later into houses. The Casa del Marqués de Salvatierra, built in the late eighteenth century, has a patio and a marble staircase of white, red and black steps. There are many paintings, among them the portraits of Espinel and of the unfortunate Architect Aldehuela who fell off his own bridge. Perhaps the finest house in Ronda is the Casa del Rey Moro, the House of the Moorish King. It was built around 1042, but is believed to be much older; perhaps it was constructed on the site of an earlier building that had disappeared. The house was beautifully restored by the aforementioned Duchess of Parcent. It was the palace of the legendary

The courtyard of the Palacio Mondragón, a Moorish-style house built in Ronda in the eighth century.

Charming views of the Casa del Marqués de Salvatierra, dating from the eighteenth century.

Once the chief mosque, Santa Maria la Mayor is now Ronda's church combining a surprisingly harmonious variety of architectural styles.

Badis, king of Tacorona (as Ronda was once called), who was infamous for his cruelty. Or it may have been the home of Al-Mutadid, former ruler of Sevilla, who amused himself by drinking wine out of the jewel-studded skulls of his victims. Similar stories are also told in other countries. Badis seems to have been a man of eccentric tastes. He was said to sleep with his aunt and people said he was crazy, though one doesn't have to be crazy to do such things.

The interior will not fascinate people who have seen the finest palaces of Spain, but there are beautiful ceramic tiles on the floors and fine old carpets. The garden is built near the very edge of the Tajo, a charming site of palms, laurels and fig trees, and with an old marble fountain. The Mina de Ronda, a staircase built into the rock, leads down to the backwater of the river where the queen once had her private pool. There are about 300 high steps, and one wonders whether the descent and later the ascent are worth the trouble. Christian slave workers cut the stairway, while others carried water up from the river. During the siege of 1485 soldiers are said to have bored a tunnel to cut off the staircase and the Moors' water supply. This seems a likely story, but the tunnel has never been found.

From the Roman Arch, an eighteenth-century gateway, and underneath the Capilla de San Miguel, perhaps the old synagogue, one sees two old bridges, the Puente Viejo, the Roman bridge, and on the right the Arab bridge. Crossing the Roman bridge one comes to the Posada de las Ánimas, the earliest inn in town, among whose guests was Cervantes. It was probably built around 1500. Only the façade survives, as on a motion picture set. The name has been explained in various ways, most of them wholly unconvincing.

For a long time, the leading hotel has been the Reina Victoria, built by an Englishman and named after Queen Victoria Eugenia, the English wife of King Alfonso XIII; she often came here to relax. For generations the hotel was the home-away-from-home for British visitors from England and especially from Gibraltar. A prominent non-British guest was the great poet, Rainer Maria Rilke. He suffered from tuberculosis and came to Ronda for the pure air and the sunshine; he died in 1926 and is now much revered. His room has been preserved, and he has a statue in the garden. His statue is not as good as his poetry, but the garden at the edge of the Tajo is beautiful and the view is magnificent. Many people go to Ronda for the view. That's the stuff dream towns are made of.

HALL IN TYROL
Austria

MILLIONS OF PEOPLE ALL OVER THE WORLD think of Austria as a dream country, but most Austrians have never been to Hall in Tyrol, their country's genuine dream town. The universal dream of Austria is composed of a baroque mixture of scenery and music, young wine and *Apfelstrudel*, operetta and Alpine skiing, and Hall has few of these attributes. It looks like a medieval stage set placed there by mistake centuries ago and since forgotten. Five miles east of Innsbruck, in the heart of the beautiful Tyrolean mountain-scape, Hall was overlooked by 'progress' until quite recently, and is still by-passed by hurried motorists on the Inntal *Autobahn* that links northern Europe with Italy. The *Autobahn* runs along the southern bank of the Inn river, and most people pay no attention to the exit leading to the picturesque town on the other side. Perhaps they wonder briefly about the copper cupolas of the old churches or the late-Gothic shape of the *Münzerturm* (Mint Tower). Little do they know that the first silver taler, forerunner of all 'dollars', was minted in this tower in 1486.

I often stopped in Hall in the 1950s on my way to or from Italy; when there was no *Autobahn* and I used the Austrian Highway No. One, which goes from the eastern border and Vienna to Lake Constance and passes right through Hall. I would leave my car at Unterer Stadtplatz, and as I got out and looked around I found myself instantly and effortlessly in the Middle Ages. The old houses were a little run down but they had character; the late-Gothic façades with bay windows and steep gables were a fine ensemble of medieval architecture. A few windows and colours were wrong but you cannot have everything. Behind were the rocky cliffs of the Karwendel Mountains, with the eight thousand-foot-high Bettelwurf. Much has been written about nearby Innsbruck, yet in the sixteenth century the *Altstadt* (Old Town) of Hall was more prosperous.

At that time Hall was surrounded by thick walls with towers and battlements. The town had been attacked by the Bavarians in 1363, 1368 and again in 1413, so the citizens had learned to defend themselves. (In 1950 when a modern sewerage system was built, they discovered that the defences had included a subterranean passage leading between the Lower and Upper Town.) From Unterer Stadtplatz I would walk up through steep, narrow streets to Oberer Stadtplatz, not so much a square as a casual arrangement of several small spaces leading into each other. St Nikolaus, the parish church

Modernization in Hall is restricted to the structures behind the façades, thus preserving the town's medieval atmosphere.

Hall in Tyrol

The Karwendel Mountains tower majestically over Austria's genuine dream town.

Langer Graben, a beautiful example of Hall's typical old world charm.

dedicated in 1281, is the dominating influence. In 1312 a high-Gothic nave was added; construction of the tower began in 1345 and ended as late as 1676. A hundred years later, the austere Gothic interior of the church was brightened up by exuberant baroque statues and ornaments.

The houses near the church are built on Gothic foundations, and though the various style mixtures are not always a joy for purists, each house somehow preserves its individual look, different from the others – the City Archive, the Town Hall, the house with the city pharmacy and the *Stubenhaus*. There are old chapels and stairways, and bizarre corners with Gothic and baroque features which help to create a beautiful harmonious ensemble. The town has less than 13,000 inhabitants. 'Hall is still small,' writes Gertrud Fussenegger who lived here for some time. 'Though the new surroundings begin to move closer toward the Old Town, Hall keeps its atmosphere. People still know one another, maybe not by name, but from meeting in the street. Here *Heimat* (hometown) is not yet a foreign word.'

Even native Austrians often confuse Hall in the Tyrol with the Hall in Styria, a summer resort near Admont, and Bad Hall in Upper Austria, a popular spa. In 1930 the Tyrolean Hall renamed itself 'Solbad Hall', taking advantage of the local thirteenth-century salt works and the old salt-water baths. A spa hotel with modern installations was set up, and for some time Hall was a health resort. But it didn't last. A few years ago the salt works had to be abandoned, the baths were closed, and to avoid confusion the Town Council in 1974 gave the place back its old name, 'Hall in Tyrol'.

Hall has been a town for almost seven hundred years, though it is actually much older. The first mention of a 'capitaneus de Halle', probably a military commander, is in a document dated 1263. In 1303, Duke Otto of Carinthia-Tyrol gave Hall *jus et nomen civitatis*; the Counts of Tyrol remained the feudal lords of Hall for several centuries. In the Middle Ages Hall was famous for its salt mines. Salt, the 'white gold', made Hall both prosperous and suspicious. To defend itself Hall needed a castle, and it eventually acquired three: Burg (Castle) Hasegg in the south, dominating the river and its navigation, of strategic importance; and the castles of Rainegg and Sparberegg in the east and west. Around 1580 the salt works employed over a thousand people, producing over 100,000 hundredweights of salt. As the salt was shipped in barrels, and salt caravans from Hall went all over Europe, the coopers of Hall became a powerful guild.

In 1477 Duke Sigismund installed the Ducal Mint in the *Münzerturm* near Castle Hasegg. Recent restoration has proved that the tower, made mostly of brick, was probably built around 1450. For several centuries the Mint of Hall was famous in Europe, producing not only the early taler but also a new half-taler and quarter-taler made of silver, as well as other coins. The taler from Hall remained for three hundred years a respected and popular means of payment all over Europe. Emperor Maximilian I of Habsburg correctly anticipated Hall's 'European' importance as a minting centre and added two crowned lions to Hall's coat-of-arms, a salt skid made of silver. After his marriage in 1494 to Bianca Maria Sforza of Milan (which added part of Italy to the Habsburg possessions) he spent his honeymoon at Castle Hasegg. Hall had a reputation of being a place where one could have a good

Hall in Tyrol

time. In 1515 Maximilian commissioned Niklas and Georg Thüring to build the beautiful St George Chapel that remains the castle's artistic *pièce de résistance*.

The sixteenth century was a great age for Hall. The imperial wedding made Hall fashionable, and several aristocrats built their castles and houses there: Aichham, Aichinger, Stolberg, Schönegg, Breitenegg and others. The Jesuits, Franciscans and other orders built convents and monasteries there. An elegant Women's Chapter, the royal *Damenstift*, added to the prestige of the town, and so, in a different way, did the local glass works whose famous artisans competed with Venice in the sixteenth century. Today Hall glasses are rare and found mostly in museums.

The Mint flourished. Its artisans were known for their solid workmanship, and they didn't cheat. The Hall taler was worth its weight in silver, which cannot be said of various dollars in use today. In 1596, a good year at the Mint, they made 360,000 talers engraved with the portrait of Ferdinand II of Habsburg. Originally the talers were stamped by hand, but European merchants were needing even more currency as trade increased so Ferdinand II ordered an engraving machine installed. The new *Silberzain* consisted of a silver band into which two rotating cylinders engraved the sovereign's portrait; the cylinders were moved by a water-wheel, the small canal for which still exists. Later the method was used in Hungary, Italy, Spain and Bohemia (modern presses were installed in the eighteenth century). Much of the silver used in Hall came from nearby mines in Schwaz, but after 1598 the Spanish armadas also brought silver from the New World. Famous minters – Ursentaler, Berdolf, König – created beautiful special coins. In 1600 Emperor Rudolf II decreed that such coins were to be kept and collected, 'not to be spent daily'. Today the Austrian Mint in Vienna occasionally produces coins for people who collect them: the numismatic passion pays off handsomely.

Life was not dull in Hall in those days. The annual fairs in spring and fall were very popular. There was much traffic on the highway to Italy and water traffic on the Inn. Coachmen, merchants, raftsmen, and the *Stesser*, strong characters at the salt works who filled the barrels, made good money and wanted entertainment. Fiddlers and minstrels made frequent appearances, and the ladies at the *Damenstift* would probably have been shocked to hear that near the Women's Tower a number of enterprising women practised the oldest profession. Disasters were frequent – fires, plague, and several earthquakes – and in 1477 the whole place almost burned down but the citizens speedily rebuilt their houses and continued having a good time. Twenty taverns and several breweries did a good business in Hall, and in 1470 a chronicler reported that wine consumption was rising steadily.

Dr Hippolyt Guarinoni from Trient (today the Italian Trento), who came to Hall in 1598 and became city physician and private doctor at the *Damenstift*, severely criticized the sybaritic habits of the inhabitants who, he complained, ate too much, bathed too long, and ran naked between their homes and the public baths. People were less inhibited in those happy days. A culinary speciality in the Tyrol, the *Speckknödel* (bacon dumplings), were said to have been 'invented' in Hall, though this is disputed elsewhere. It is

One of the picturesque churches which is a landmark in Hall.

said that a woman cook at the Three Lilies tavern made round dumplings of a mixture of flour, bread, bacon, sausage, eggs and milk 'to remind her soldier-guests of cannon balls'. Tyrolean peasants now love their dumplings and eat them on Tuesdays, Thursdays and Sundays. Though in 1607 'three hundred babies died, having been fed one and a half litres of milk several times a day', life was pleasant enough to attract important people, among them the executioner of Tyrol. In 1651 the castellan of nearby Rattenberg, which claims to be the oldest town in Austria, dined at the Goldenes Kreuz tavern in Hall; he sent for the executioner, a gentleman named Krieger, and informed him he would have to behead his chancellor Bienner two days later. The executioner's wife found out about it and warned Bienner, who got away and saved his neck. No one listened to Dr Guarinoni, who implored the citizens to mix their wine with water. On a somewhat higher level Guarinoni and his friends Ritter Florian von Waldauf (a personal friend of the emperor) and Dr Johannes Fuchsmagen founded the *Haller Stubengesellschaft*, which began as a convivial drinking group but later became a cultural society. The *Europäerkreis* – the circle of Europeans – in Hall kept in touch with humanists all over the continent. Dr Guarinoni, much revered in Hall today, loved the town, 'which surpasses in grace and content all other towns in the country'.

In 1573 the Jesuits founded a gymnasium in Hall. They had to leave two hundred years later, but the secondary school survives to this day, one of the oldest in Europe. Hall even came close to having its own university. Its *Fasnachtsspiel* (carnival) has been popular since the fourteenth century, and the orchestra of the *Damenstift* was the second best in the Tyrol, after the *Hofmusik* of Innsbruck.

Jacob Stainer was born, probably around 1617, in the nearby village of Absam; he is known as the greatest non-Italian violin-maker. Unlike the great masters in Cremona, Stainer was not a good businessman. He would sell his instruments for about four talers to merchants who came with the salt

Hall's beautiful old churches, impressive in themselves, take on a dream-like quality from the landscape.

caravans to Hall, and never got more than twenty-four guilders for a very fine fiddle. He died poor and sick in Absam in 1683. A hundred years later collectors in Europe valued a Stainer violin at four times the price of a Stradivari.

Hall's connection with the world's great musicians extends further: on 26 October 1772 Wolfgang Amadeus Mozart, then sixteen, performed on the beautiful organ at the Stiftskirche while on a visit there with his father. Later the organ was sold to the church in Fügen, in the Zillertal.

Hall's glory ended in 1809 when the Mint was closed by the Bavarians. After the railroad was built Hall also lost its importance as a river port and trans-shipment centre; the last ship for Vienna left in 1872. The town became quiet and a little run down. The final blow was the end of the salt works and spa installations in 1967. But in the past few years the wheel of local history has been turned around once more. Innsbruck expanded as an industrial and international tourist centre, so that its eastern suburbs almost reach Hall, which was 'rediscovered'.

Hall was always an artistically-minded town. The frescoes at the St Nikolaus Church are among the outstanding works of early fresco painting in the Tyrol. Renowned artists laboured at the glass works, among local architects and at the Mint. The Tyrolean baroque painters, Christoph Anton Mayr and Josef Adam Mölk, worked in local churches and convents. Franz Borgias Stöckl, Christoph Wörndle, Gregor Fritz and Josef and Georg Walch contributed fine sculptures and altars. Although there was little artistic life in the somnolent nineteenth century, later artists have worked here: Franz Xaver Fuchs, Josef Bachlechner Jun., Helmut and Maria Rehm, Imre Seilern, Peter Prandstetter and Anton Tiefenthaler. Max Weiler, born in Absam in 1910, who painted frescoes at the school he attended in Hall, is one of Austria's foremost abstract painters and teaches at Vienna's Akademie der bildenden Künste.

In past years Castle Hasegg has been restored, and many of the old houses in Hall have had their façades repaired and painted. Modern apartments are created behind old façades: it is fashionable to live in an old house, preferably with modern plumbing. The *Münzerturm* has been restored. In 1975 the modernized Mint was reopened after 167 years of Sleeping Beauty existence. In the same year the Mint in Hall produced half of all the Olympic 100-schilling coins (the other half was minted in Vienna). The Numismatic Society of the Tyrol and Town Council of Hall have great plans for the future. They hope to make Castle Hasegg and the *Münzerturm* a permanent numismatic museum showing the historical coins minted in Hall, with a reference library and other features such as studios for artists. They want to make Hall 'the Mecca of numismatics'. In 1977 the Mint will celebrate its five-hundredth anniversary. Perhaps the Republic of Austria will allow Hall to produce a memorial coin with as much significance for Europe as its first taler.

BRUGES
West Flanders, Belgium

RUGES (BRUGGE) IS A TOWN of dramatic contradictions. Once capital of a rich region, Bruges lost much wealth and power in the sixteenth century and became Bruges-la-Morte, The Dead City, as the novelist Rodenbach called it in 1892. But no city likes to be declared dead, and the people of Bruges resent the cliché; neither do they want their city to be called 'the Venice of the North'. Bruges has, in fact, survived its downfall and its cliches and presents itself today as very much alive, yet conscious of the grandeur of its past, which is not a bad combination.

Bruges's tragedy has been the world's gain. For when Bruges was demoted by an invincible combination of geographic, economic and social forces, the town suddenly fell asleep – for centuries. Had its decline been more gradual, its medieval beauty would have been slowly eroded, and the beautiful old façades might have been replaced by far less beautiful modern structures. For centuries Bruges remained forgotten, bypassed by history, and thus remained a jewel of medieval mysticism. The people of Bruges now talk mostly of the future as people do elsewhere, but they are happy that their past turns out to give an unexpected bonus: the modern gold mine of tourism.

It's useful to keep in mind that the grandeur of Bruges was both created and finally destroyed by the sea. Its beginnings go back to Baudoin 1, Count of Flanders, who built his castle – a castle meant power – near a bridge in the ninth century. Bruges is named after 'brugge', the Flemish word for bridge, or possibly after the Scandinavian 'bryggja', meaning pier or landing place. It had thick walls and four gates, called Holy Cross, Ostend, Ghent and Maréchale. In the eleventh century the Reye linked the town with the Zwyn, the outer harbour of Damme, and eventually with the North Sea. Bruges became an important trans-shipment point for vessels from all over Europe. Flemish artisans brought cloth, the English their wool, and the Scandinavians cod and herring. From Bordeaux and the Loire came wines, from the Baltic Sea, grains, from Bohemia and the Carpathian Mountains, copper. Venetian galleys and ships from Genoa brought spices and other treasures of the Orient. Lombardy sent gold brocades.

No wonder then that Bruges became attractive to the shrewd Hanseatic merchants in Lübeck and Bremen who set up a *Kontor* (trade headquarters) in Bruges and for a long time carried on a fabulous business.

Quays or benches from which one can enjoy sights like this line the canals in Bruges.

*The scene which probably inspired
Henry Wadsworth Longfellow to write
The Belfry of Bruges.*

They never controlled the trade though, as they did elsewhere. The merchants and bankers of Bruges wisely kept control for themselves. They remained managers of the foreign trade missions. Numerous protectionist rules established the dominant position of local families, who became rich and powerful. The preserved thirteenth-century journal of a merchant shows commercial relations of his firm extending to over thirty countries. As many as 150 vessels would arrive on one day at Damme or at Minnewater (Lac d'Amour), the commercial basin formed by the river Reye.

Bruges was certainly not 'dead' in those days; on the contrary, wealth and power brought jealousy and violence. In 1127 Charles the Good, Count of Flanders, was assassinated in Saint Donatiens Church while praying. He had aroused the hatred of his courtiers under his Chancellor Erembaud. The assassins barricaded themselves in the church and only surrendered seven weeks later. The church has since disappeared, but its outlines can be seen in Place du Bourg, then centre of the old town, where the rulers had their castle and their church.

Violence has continued in Bruges, where burghers and guilds were powerful and proud of their independence. The Léliaerts (Gens du Lys) stood behind the Kings of France while the Clauwaerts (Gens de la Griffe) remained faithful to the Counts of Flanders. In 1301 King Philip IV (the Fair) felt 'obliged' to intervene. He had Guy de Dampierre, Count of Flanders, arrested and then visited Bruges. His wife, Queen Jeanne, was surprised by the elegantly dressed women of Bruges: 'I thought I was the only queen but I saw a hundred others around me,' she said. When in 1429 Philip the Good welcomed his fiancée, Isabella of Portugal, in Bruges, the reception was an affair *de grande luxe*; it was said no house in Bruges lacked expensive silverware. During the celebrations Philip had himself promoted to Grand Duke of the Occident (becoming the first prince of his time) and founded the Order of the Golden Fleece. This later passed to the Habsburgs when they gained control of the Burgundian possessions.

The Habsburgs, who wisely preferred marriages to wars, achieved their objective when Emperor Maximilian I married Maria of Burgundy, daughter of Charles the Bold. Maria died at the age of twenty-five after a fall from her horse, and Maximilian was free to marry again. His expansionist marriage policies were aptly summed up by King Matthias Corvinus of Hungary, '*Bella gerant alii; tu, felix Austria, nube*' (Let others wage war; you, lucky Austria, marry).

The fifteenth century was the golden age in and of Bruges, and plenty of gold passed through the town, where rich merchants, shipping magnates and bankers commissioned artists and artisans, painters and woodworkers, sculptors and architects to make their hometown more beautiful than ever. The rich had money and taste and wanted to make their town a showcase of medieval art. Bruges developed its own style of architecture, with gilded façades, rectangular windows and tympanums above. The great Belfry of Bruges, symbol of the burghers' pride and power, is perhaps the most beautiful in Belgium – an 83 metre (275-foot) high tower that reaches out of the centre of the Halles and dominates the town. Its square lower part was built after 1282, while the upper octagonal part was added in 1482

LEFT *The Chapel of the Holy Blood is said to house a phial containing several drops of Christ's blood, presented in 1150 by the Patriarch of Jerusalem to Dierick of Alsace, Count of Flanders, in honour of his courageous part in the Crusades.*
RIGHT *The Hospital of St John is an unspoilt example of Bruges twelfth-century architecture; it is still used as a hospital but also houses the Memling Museum and one of the oldest pharmacies in the world.*

when the famous carillon was installed; 366 steps lead up to the top from where one has a magnificent view. The statues on the façade of the Halles and the former Aldermen's House are not the original ones, which were destroyed during the French Revolution. Fortunately the revolutionaries failed to destroy the fine Gothic hanging vault inside.

Bruges was always a pious city, Bruges-la-Pieuse, and its heart was in Place du Bourg where the town's greatest relic is kept. After the Second Crusade, Thierry d'Alsace brought the Relic of the Holy Blood, an ampoule with a few drops of the blood of Christ, gathered by Joseph of Arimathea, from the Holy Land to Bruges. The Basilica of the Holy Blood, a Romanesque underchurch or crypt, the twelfth-century Chapel of St Basil, and above a fifteenth-century Chapel of the Holy Blood, with a flamboyant Renaissance entrance, house the relic in its beautiful baroque silver

Bruges

ABOVE *Fine Old Flemish houses border the Grande Place.*
LEFT *The beautiful fifteenth-century Gruuthuse Mansion, originally the home of wealthy merchants, is now a museum.*

container. Each year on the Monday following 2 May the relic is carried around Bruges in a ceremony suggesting medieval mysticism. Every five years, the Play of the Holy Blood – a series of tableaux inspired by the Bible – is performed by local people against the fine background of the Halles and the Belfry. Near the Basilica are the Town Hall, the Renaissance Franc (the former Recorder's Office), and the Palais de Justice, formerly known as Palace du Franc. Its façade is a mixture of Gothic and Renaissance elements, and its famous fireplace is made of black marble, oak wood and an alabaster frieze made by Lancelot Blondeel, a local all-round genius – painter, sculptor, architect, engineer – who has been compared to Leonardo da Vinci. The main statue shows Charles Quint.

The wealthy merchants had splendid residences built for themselves. The Gruuthuse, once the home of the Lords of Gruuthuse, is now an archaeological museum recalling the early history of Flanders. The merchants of Genoa had a fine house showing St George and the dragon. J. van de Poele built a house in Square Memling. The van Buerse family, in whose house in Grouwwerkstraat local merchants and bankers would meet to trade and make their deals, later gave the language the expression 'bourse', or stock

The main entrance to the béquinage (above) is over an old bridge
across one of the picturesque canals that criss-cross the city.
Bruges' béquinage is one of the finest in Belgium ; originally
a retreat for secular nuns it now houses a religious order.

exchange. From the courtyard of the Gruuthuse one has a fine view of Notre Dame Church, the most beautiful in Bruges. Its foundations go back to the ninth century, but most of the church was built in the thirteenth century, a remarkable blend of Romanesque, Gothic and Renaissance elements with a fine brick tower and many art treasures inside. The most important is an early pietà by Michelangelo, made around 1503, given to the church by a rich citizen, Jean de Mouscron. The beautiful statues on seventeenth-century pillars are works of Gaspard de Crayer, Pierre Pourbus, Bernard van Orley and Gérard David. Underneath are the sarcophagi of Charles the Bold and Maria of Burgundy.

Also part of the pious town are the houses, gardens and fourteenth-century church of the Beguines. Their order, set up in the thirteenth century, was later replaced by Benedictine nuns from the Vigne Convent. This is really a town within the town, surrounded by silent trees and quiet canals. It has been said that in Bruges, in the middle of silence, there are certain spots that are even more profoundly silent. The famous canals of Bruges that created the comparison with Venice have attracted people for centuries. Their banks have poetic names – Quai Vert, Quai Rosaire, Quai du Mirroir – recalling the past. White swans swim majestically on the black waters, and they too have their legend in Bruges. After the assassination in 1488 of Pierre Langhals, an unpopular adviser of Emperor Maximilian, the citizens were ordered to care for the swans, or else.

Bruges

The best is yet to come. The fifteenth century gave Bruges the master-pieces of its greatest painters – Jan Van Eyck, Van der Goes, Hans Memling, Petrus Christus, Jean Provost, Gérard Davis and several anonymous masters. Their paintings are at the Musée Groeninge, also known as Musée Communal des Beaux Arts. The museum is well organized, with one hall given to the works of Van Eyck, another to Van der Goes, and one to Memling and two unknown painters. Memling remains the most important artist in Bruges: he is to Bruges what Rubens is to Antwerp. The finest things he did are the frescoes for the Saint Jean Hospital, a fine twelfth-century building with a Romanesque sick room and pharmacy and a sixteenth-century cloister. Memling's *The Shrine of Sainte Ursula* shows in astonishing, always poetic detail the martyrdom of the holy woman. Memling is said to have painted these fantastic frescoes to show his gratitude for the good treatment he received at the hospital as a wounded soldier, from a pious nun. He, in turn, has taken good care of the former hospital. The incredible mystical beauty of his paintings cannot be described in words; it can only be felt.

Bruges seems to have affected all artists who created there. Even the so-called Jerusalem Church of 1492, inspired by the Church of the Holy Sepulchre in Jerusalem, emerged as a work of the medieval art of Bruges with its unique nave and strange choir. The builders, Pierre and Jacques Afornes, went several times to Jerusalem to study the church there, but the Jerusalem Church is more Bruges than Jerusalem.

In the sixteenth century Bruges, then rich and powerful and perhaps insolent and frivolous, was struck by tragedy. The Zwyn and the canals were filled with sand brought in by violent floods. The terrified Brugeois tried all they could to avert disaster and keep the vital canals open. Lancelot Blondeel designed a new canal, but he was centuries ahead of his time. Gradually the Zwyn became a vast creek, silted up and silent. (It now forms the frontier between Belgium and Holland.) For a while the outside harbour of Damme profited from the decline of Bruges. A monumental church, built there in 1230, burned down in 1578; only the nave remains. Charles the Bold had married Marguerite of York there in 1486. But then he went to Bruges, where the action and the fun were, to celebrate.

Under Philip II the power of Bruges came to its inexorable end. Had they been able to save the port, it might have competed with Antwerp. But the rich merchants of Bruges completed the tragedy of their town that nature had begun. They wouldn't let the English bring in their expensive textiles, so the English took their trade to Ghent and later to Antwerp. On a day in 1457, sixty-six vessels had arrived in Bruges, bringing in 6500 tons of goods. By 1499 there were only twenty-three arrivals on one day, and the decline continued fast. One by one the great houses were forced to close. The last to leave, in 1546, were the Hanseatic merchants. Bruges was finished and became a melancholy expression of medieval romanticism, a sort of Florence where everything formed an ensemble of timeless beauty – churches and houses, trees and canals. Then Bruges fell asleep.

In 1907 a new canal was completed – almost an exact copy of the design of Blondeel, centuries earlier – that linked Bruges with Zeebrugge (the

Lace-making is a traditional occupation in Bruges.

Flemish word for Brugge-by-the-Sea). Today Greater Brugge has 110,000 inhabitants and is an important seaport and centre of technology, with institutes of learning, a place for lace-making and, above all, a great attraction for travellers from everywhere. It takes a little searching, but eventually visitors discover Bruges-la-Morte, the old town of the past, mystical and melancholy, silent and lovely. It is very beautiful. Along the canals one can smell the scent of the nearby sea, and at night, the old people say, one can hear the sound of the phantom vessels disappearing into the sand.

DELFT
South Holland, The Netherlands

DELFT, SYNONYMOUS WITH CHINA, Blue Delftware or just blue, is really much more. Johannes Vermeer was born and died in Delft, and Pieter de Hoogh created his finest works there. In the seventeenth century, Delft's Golden Age, it was truly a painters' town. To the Dutch, Delft means history, the place where William of Orange, 'Father of the Fatherland', was assassinated, and remains venerated as the burial place of their Royal Family. And to the world at large, the lovely old districts of Delft have preserved the intimate charm of past centuries better than any other place in the Netherlands.

If you take the trouble to find it. 'Though Delft has become big – it is one of Holland's medium-sized cities – its old centre can still, at quiet times of the day, transport you back in spirit to the distant past, and the best time is very early in the morning, preferably on a Sunday', writes Jan H. Oosterloo, who knows and loves Delft. The name comes from 'Delf' ('ditch'), specifically the canal dug in the post-Roman era linking Corbulo's canal with the Lede, now called the Schie. Thus an inhabitant of Delft today calls himself *Delvenaar*, not *Delftenaar*. The beginnings of Delft are lost in darkness (and some argument), but it is mentioned as a small hamlet as early as 989 AD. It may have been a Roman settlement located between two watchtowers on the banks of the Oude (Old) Delft canal. Late in the eleventh century Godfried van Lotharingen (known as Govert the Hunchback) built his castle exactly where the Town Hall of Delft now stands. Govert later surrounded the hamlet with canals and ramparts, and made Delft 'Govaerts Veste' (Govert's Fortress).

In 1246 Delft received municipal rights from William II of Orange. At that time Delft already had its Thursday markets for agricultural produce of the region. The custom has remained. Every Thursday is Market Day in the Markt, possibly the most beautiful square in the Netherlands, dominated by the New Church at one end and the Town Hall at the other. On such days the Markt is filled with noise and people, stalls and goods. One is reminded that Delft started its career as the centre of a farming district. Today the descendants of earlier farmers sit around in the cafés near the Beestenmarkt (cattle market) while their wives do the weekly shopping in town.

For the visitors the most picturesque Thursday event is the flower market in the old town, along the banks of Voldersgracht and Hippolytusbuurt,

Near-perfect reflections in the tranquil Oude Delft canal.

Delft

where painters often put up their easels. There are stalls full of flowers, the joy and pride of Holland. The amazing Dutch always have flowers. In spring there are varieties of tulips, hyacinths and daffodils; long before you can see them, you smell their fragrance along the canals. In summertime there are roses and carnations, and later in fall asters, red dahlias and chrysanthemums.

From eleven o'clock until noon, the forty-eight-bell carillon is played on top of the Gothic tower of Nieuwe Kerk (New Church), and then the mood of Old Delft becomes strong. The carillon is also played on Tuesday and Saturday mornings, and in summertime on Tuesday evenings, by local carilloneurs and guest performers. On warm nights they place chairs in the square, and the people sit and listen. If they close their eyes and use some imagination, they may find themselves back in Delft's great past. The past remains strong in Delft though some have been working overtime trying to ruin it. Some of the old ramparts have disappeared, and it was planned to fill in the lovely Oude Delft canal to place the streetcar trains there. After much protest the canal was saved, but the ramparts on the western side of the old town had to be sacrificed to the exigencies of modern traffic. Some people like the fast electric trains leaving every few minutes for The Hague (5 miles) and Rotterdam (8 miles) better than the promenades along the tree-lined canals, which have black waters in wintertime and transparently green ones in summer, the fine quay of the Koornmarkt, the covered foot-bridges with high steps, the façades of old houses – all the things that give the old town of Delft its indelible imprint. The former watchtowers survive only on the town's coat-of-arms.

At the end of the Oude Delft, in a small garden near the former Hague Gate, is a famous grave surrounded by wrought-iron railings ornamented with fleurs-de-lis. The grave contains Delft's best-known mystery. According to the tombstone, Louis XVII, also known as Charles Louis, Duke of Normandy, King of France and Navarre, is buried there – but is he? The death of the Dauphin, son of Louis XVI and Marie-Antoinette, at the Temple prison in Paris in 1793 has never been proved. Under the reign of Louis XVIII several pretenders claimed to be sons of the unfortunate couple and thus to have the right to sit on the throne of France. The most convincing among them was a certain Naundorff, a watchmaker, who was surrounded by a group of intimates. They were impressed by the accuracy of his reminiscences and recognized him as the legitimate sovereign until he died in Delft, on 10 August 1845. In the autumn of 1950 the vault had to be renovated, and the bones were inspected by experts. They revealed no clues concerning the true identity, if any, of 'Naundorff'. And the Last Will of the Duchess of Angoulême, which might have revealed some important facts, has never been found. Delft is happy to keep its mystery.

Delft offers other puzzles. The New Church was called 'new' to distinguish it from Oude Kerk, the 'Old' Church, once a small wooden structure, later a stone church, known for its leaning tower and Bourdon bell. The not-so-new New Church dates from 1381 when Albrecht van Beyeren gave permission to build a church dedicated to the Holy Virgin. Later it was called Sainte Ursula Church. Originally it also was made of wood. Behind

The colour applied to Delft ware is initially black, not blue; after painting, the pottery is glazed and is fired again. This pottery, at the stage of second firing, will take on the characteristic Delft blue colour.

162

ABOVE *Clay on the potter's wheel in the first stage of becoming another fine piece of famous Delft ware which will bear a State guarantee.*

LEFT *Delft ware is entirely hand made; this craftsman paints a traditional design which could be one of those imitated from the early Japanese or Chinese originals which were the prototypes for Delft ware.*

RIGHT *A beautiful selection of finished Delft ware.*

the church is a lovely canal called Vrouwenrecht, 'Women's Rights'. They had them in Delft long before Women's Lib. Gradually the tower was built and the clockwork put in. In 1441 lightning destroyed the thatched top of the tower. The sturdy Netherlanders didn't give up and after a while the tower was finished – in 1496. In 1663 the carillon, made by Franciscus Hemno, was installed. 'Whenever you hear the clear sound of the chimes, remember your last day on earth.' On 29 September 1872 the tower was again struck by lightning. A complete restoration of the church was finished shortly before the Second World War. The most recent restoration was completed in 1950 – but will it be the last?

The New Church is a national monument in the Netherlands. It is very beautiful in late-Gothic, with the mausoleum of William I of Orange (William the Silent) in the choir. Hendrik de Keyzer began work on it in 1614. The thrifty Dutch remember that it cost 34,000 guilders, a fortune really, and was finished only in 1622, two years after the builder's death. The burial vault of the House of Orange is underneath the choir. It cannot be visited but one is informed that the crypt has had to be enlarged twice already, and that the Father of the Fatherland rests exactly under his monument in the choir.

Sint Agathaklooster, founded in 1402 as a women's convent, became the residence of the first William in 1572. Later the town of Delft gave William the building as a gift. On 10 July 1584 he was assassinated there by Balthasar Gerars. The spot where the bullets struck him was later marked in the wall and the place is now a shrine. After the death of William I, the Princes of Orange stayed there. In 1667 the house was the home of two grandchildren of William, the princesses of Portugal. But then the Prinsenhof began to deteriorate. For a while it was used as a cloth exchange and as a school, and towards the end of the eighteenth century the residence of the Father Willem became an army barracks, which is pretty bad, as anyone will admit who has lived in army barracks.

In 1883 the Dutch government decided to restore the Prinsenhof, but there wasn't enough money to do a thorough job, and only the historic hall was renovated and reopened in 1887. Finally, in 1948 – the anniversary of the Peace Treaty of Münster that marked the end of the long war against Spain – the Prinsenhof was completely restored. It is a labyrinth of halls and corridors with crossbeam ceilings and winding staircases. It is now the Stedelijk Museum (Municipal Museum), and has 'the special and exclusive atmosphere which is and always has been so characteristic of Delft' (Oosterloo). Late in October the annual Art and Antique Dealers' Fair is held there.

And if the 'special atmosphere' seems somehow familiar to you, this is no accident. It was this special atmosphere that Vermeer caught in his paintings so beautifully three hundred years ago. At the Paul Tetar van Elven Museum, at Koornmarkt 67, there is an artist's studio 'in the old Dutch manner' that could have been used by Vermeer. This brings up a sad, often mentioned complaint. Not a single work of Delft's greatest painter is kept in his hometown. For a long time, the town of Cremona suffered a similar indignity; it didn't have a single one of the great violins that had

A stretch of the lovely tree-lined canal of old Delft.

been made there. Delft's loss was felt particularly in the winter of 1950 when Vermeer's *Sight of Delft* hung temporarily in the Prinsenhof because the Mauritshuis Museum in The Hague was closed for repairs. Local experts – and not only they – said wistfully that never before had Vermeer's masterpiece seemed more beautiful. The Delft school of painting was indicated by Meester van Delft, Maerten van Heemskerck and Jacob Delff de Oude, and really began with the great portrait painters Jacob Delff de Jonge, Willem Willemsz van Vliet and Jan Daemen Cool; it continued with the still-life painters Evert and Willem van Aelst and Balthasar van der Ast, and later with Anthonie Palamedesz, Paulus Potter, Cornelis van Vliet, Emanuel Witte and Rembrandt's pupil, Carel Fabritius. Then came Vermeer and Pieter de Hoogh. Jan Steen lived for a few years in Delft, as manager of the beer brewery De Slange in Oude Delft, but he was not a member of Sint Lucasgilde (the St Luke's Guild) to which the artists of Delft belonged. Its last important members were Egbert van der Poel and Jan Verkolje. Then the decline of Delft set in and lasted for a long time. Around 1900 Delft had only 13,000 inhabitants; today there are over 80,000 people.

Beer brewing began in the thirteenth century and became an important industry in Delft when local beer was exported to Flanders and later to Germany. Apparently the soft water in the canals of Delft was well suited to the production of beer. In the fifteenth century the town had over two hundred large and small breweries. Cloth-weaving also became of major importance and today some street names – Voldersgracht (Fullers' Canal) and Verwersdijk (Dyers' Dyke) – prove it. In the sixteenth century Flemish refugees imported the art of making fine tapestries. Finally the faience industry became prominent; it had its ups and downs but gloriously survives to this day.

Originally pottery in Delft followed the traditional majolica patterns of the southern Netherlands or, more exactly, of Italian majolica. Italian potters had settled in the late sixteenth century in France and Belgium. Then Portuguese seamen brought specimens of Chinese porcelain to western Europe. In the Low Countries the Chinese products were much admired. Marco Polo had earlier brought some porcelain from China, and 'soft' porcelain (which wasn't porcelain at all) was made in Florence under the Medicis around 1575. After the Dutch West and East India Companies were founded, with headquarters in Delft, the Dutch began importing the blue-and-white porcelain of the Late Ming era and the Wan-Li ware. The Dutch potters imported the Chinese products, but they didn't know the art of making porcelain; their products had neither the brilliance nor the translucence of genuine porcelain. In the early seventeenth century over thirty potteries were busy in Delft, among them De Porceleyne Fles (The Porcelain Bottle), established in 1653. They made mostly blue-and-white products but coloured tiles in green, orange, yellow and violet were also quite popular. The potters claimed to make a product which was 'almost as good' as porcelain; the Dutch painters began to develop their own style.

In 1707 Johann Friedrich Böttger, after long, hard years of experimenting, invented the art of making porcelain in Saxony. During the following

LEFT *Fishing vessels moored in the smaller of Bergen's two harbours.* BELOW LEFT *Bergen's timber houses have been renewed but, in many cases, the actual ground plan is very old, dating from medieval times.*

Delft

decades porcelain factories were founded in Meissen, Berlin, Nymphenburg, Sèvres, and elsewhere. In Staffordshire, England, Josiah Wedgwood made a white pottery body that didn't need the opaque white enamel covering and permitted the application of a better painting technique; Wedgwood's pottery was also less brittle. But the Dutch were unable to imitate the new products from Saxony and England, much as they tried. To begin with, they didn't have the right clays or other materials; no white burning clays are found in Holland. To beat the competition the Dutch began to produce cheaper pottery. That was a mistake. They worked in a hurry, the designs deteriorated, and many potteries had to close down. At the time of the Liberation from the French in 1813, only three potteries operated in Delft, among them De Porceleyne Fles, and finally it was the only one to survive, though barely, during the first half of the eighteenth century.

In 1876 Joost Thooft started the renaissance. Together with an expert called Labouchère he made a new type of blue Delft with the hard body of Wedgwood pottery. The white burning clays were mixed, then the various objects – plates and vases – were shaped, either on the potter's wheel or in plastic moulds, and were then dried and fired. The decorations were painted by hand, and the objects were glazed and fired for a second time. At that point the paintings were dull-black, not blue, but after the second firing (glost fire) they re-emerged in the special shade of blue for which Delft became famous. It took some time to find the right methods, the exact temperatures, and able artists, but Thooft and Labouchère succeeded.

Genuine Blue Delftware has a triple signature: a plump vase topped by a straight line, and underneath the stylized letter F and the word 'Delft'. The special cracked quality of this pottery is achieved after some additional bakings. They don't like to give away their secrets, and you must not blame them. Not all Delft is blue, however. A rich red glaze was introduced in 1948, and now they make pottery in green, gold and black that is reminiscent of Persian tapestries. The making of 'Royal Delft', as it is now called, can be seen on every weekday from early April until late October at the Royal Delftware Manufactory at 196 Rotterdamseweg. There is also a permanent exhibition of fine and beautiful Delftware, old and new.

Blue Delftware has, in fact, become part of the modern Delft, now an important town of science and industry, with 9000 students at the local technological university, and with important scientific institutions. They continue the work of Delft's Golden Age scientists, Hugo Grotius (Hugo de Groot) and Anthonie van Leeuwenhoek. Along the old Rotterdam Road there are modern buildings, laboratories and that symbol of our age, a nuclear reactor. But behind the façade of the modern city remains Oude Delft, the blue flower of Delft romanticism.

BERGEN
Hordaland, Norway

U NLIKE MANY DREAM TOWNS, Bergen has both an airport and a railroad station, but to get that all-important first impression of sheer magic you should arrive by boat, preferably at dawn. That may be difficult to manage, but it's worth the trouble: Norway is a sea country and the sea helps you to understand the cold vastness of it. Few of the four million Norwegians live more than forty miles away from the sea. Norway's wealth always came from the ocean. First it was whale and cod, then it was trade; soon it will be oil. Seven-tenths of Norway is rock and glacier, mountains and woods, and many wonderful dramatic views – but when North Sea oil begins to flow in quantities, the Norwegians will be among the richest people in Europe.

In some ways they've always been rich. Their fjord country is one of the wonders of the world. And a fine place to start from on that scenic journey is Bergen, evergreen and always lovely, on a peninsula with a double harbour and with a half circle of mountains behind it. Somewhat like Rome, Bergen is located on seven hills; its coat of arms is a castle with seven angels. The coastline of Norway is wild and rugged, but the harbour of Bergen is protected by small islands and kept relatively mild by the Gulf Stream, known in Bergen as the North Atlantic drift.

It doesn't just rain in Bergen; they have different kinds of rain and are specific about it like the *Bordelais* about their wines. They have a sort of dusty rain, fine, with pinpricks; rain that comes down in barrels; steady, slow rain, almost as in Salzburg, that has a soporific effect on people; and a rainy wind (or windy rain), sweeping the streets. There is also the terrifying rain that makes some people think of the imminent end of the world, when sheets of water reach down from sky to earth, or possibly from the fjords to the skies; it's hard to tell the difference. They claim they even have an invisible rain that you don't see but quite definitely feel. Amazingly, the people of Bergen love their rains and wouldn't want to live without them. One of the many rainy stories told in Bergen is about the boy who is asked by a foreigner whether it always rains like that. 'I wouldn't know,' he says. 'I am only eight years old.' That's supposed to be very funny in Bergen.

They also tell you that the horses in the street may shy when they see someone who isn't holding an umbrella. There are citizens who recall unhappily the sunny days and blue skies of Italy or Provence where they

The small fishing boats and the quayside flower stalls create a charming atmosphere in this Bergen scene.

Situated on a double peninsula in a mountainous fjord province Bergen looks out on a dramatic landscape around lake Store Lungegårdsvann.

went for their holidays. Never again, they say. It was terrible, no rain at all. But there is something invigorating about the healthy climate of Bergen. It's rarely very cold. In summertime the rhododendron is plentiful, and even the warmest days are never hot or humid. New York City was never like that.

Bergen has much rain, but it has also had many fires in its long history. In 1702 almost the whole town burned down. In January 1916 the heart of the city, between Vaagen and Lungegard, went up in flames. Most of the older houses were built of wood and burned like candles. The wide sidestreets, called *almenninger*, are medieval fire ditches, but often they didn't prevent the flames from leaping across them when the winds were strong. The centre of Bergen, Torvalmenningen, the widest street in Norway, is such a former fire ditch.

Bergen was founded in 1070 AD by King Olaf III Haraldsson, called the Quiet (or the Peaceful) to distinguish him from other kings who were neither quiet nor peaceful. Survival was never easy in the rugged homeland of the Vikings. Olaf II pressed to establish Christianity in his land of pagans, was driven into exile by Canute the Great in 1028 AD, and returned two years later to reconquer Norway. Eventually Norway became a Christian, God-fearing land, and Olaf became a martyr and a saint. The Saint Olaf Monastery in Bergen is called after *him*, not after the peaceful founder, known in the textbooks as King Olav Kyrri. Recent archaeological discoveries have raised doubts as to whether Bergen was founded in 1070; at any rate, they celebrated their nine hundredth anniversary in 1970. Originally Bergen was called Björgvin, 'the meadow between the mountains'. The founder is credited with laying the foundations of Christ Church and Hakonshallen (King Haakon's Hall), almost destroyed by fire in 1944 and later restored.

That was of course after the legendary Vikings raided and occupied a considerable part of England and sailed their ships to Iceland, Greenland and all the way to America, Spain, Portugal and even to Constantinople. At the time of the Norman invasion of England, the early Bergen was well situated for trade, and the town prospered. The kings of Norway, who had been crowned in Trondheim, moved to Bergen which was the country's capital in the thirteenth century. The *Thing*, predecessor of Norway's Parliament, called *Storting*, was in Bergen. From 1381 until 1814, Norge (Norway) was united with Denmark, from 1815 until 1905 with Sweden. Then the Swedish union was dissolved, and a Danish prince became King Haakon VII of Norway. Norway is now a constitutional monarchy.

Over a century ago, the sea lanes were Bergen's only communication with the outside world. There was no highway from Bergen to Oslo, no railroad to Kristiania. By sailboat it took at least ten days to go from Bergen to Oslo, but only a few days to the east coast of England or to the cities of northern Germany. The sea lanes were both a blessing and the cause of Bergen's historical tragedy: the merchants of the German Hansa knew a good thing when they saw it. They moved in; by the end of the thirteenth century they were firmly established. They were real occupiers who had their own district of Bryggen, on the eastern bank of the old port of Vaagen.

Bergen

After London, Bruges in Belgium and Novgorod, Bergen became the fourth great Hanseatic settlement. From the fourteenth to the middle of the seventeenth century, the Hansa merchants had their *Kontor* and *Faktorei* (the medieval merchants' guild) in Bergen. Many German merchants sent their sons there for their apprenticeship.

The Hanseatic Museum, formerly a merchant's house on the German Quay, now Bryggen (The Quay), displays the boards with the twelve commandments for apprentices. Apprentices caught breaking a commandment were flogged with ropes that had nails fixed to them. The ropes are also displayed, for those who would call the whole story 'mere propaganda'. Hans Jürgen Hansen, a German publisher, admits 'the Hanseatic history in Bergen had its dark, embarrassing (*peinliche*) aspects but basically the Norwegians in Bergen didn't have a worse life than people elsewhere in Europe wno depended on the rule of the patricians. In the fourteenth and fifteenth centuries, things were rough all over Europe, not only in Bergen. . . .'

The League had a firm monopoly on dried codfish and the herring trade, and on salt from Lüneburg – very important since salt was expensive, costing half as much as butter, and was needed for the curing and pickling of many foodstuffs. The Hansa merchants also dominated the fur trade, and furs were much in demand since the houses in northern Europe were rarely heated. Other monopolies of the Hanseatic League were textiles from England, timber and wax from Russia, beer from Hamburg, ceramics from Germany, and Oriental spices from Bruges. The Hansa merchants had sufficient capital and their own ships, and they worked with methods that seem modern even now. Around 1750 the last Hanseatic *Kontor* was abolished; by that time the German merchants had lost much of their political power as well as many monopolies. The history of Bergen remains an argument among historians, depending on whether they belong to the older national-romantic school, or to the newer enlightened school. Apparently the Hanseatic merchants were not selective in their methods; at the Hanseatic Museum one sees their scales that had two sets of weights – one for buying, one for selling. It is also a fact that the Norwegian merchants took over where the Germans left off. Bergen survived, and many people claim that the town profited from the supposedly dark, Hanseatic past. By the end of the nineteenth century, Norway was the world's fourth-largest shipping nation. Today the country's merchant marine fleet is the fifth-largest and its earnings help to offset the unfavourable trade balance.

The Old Town in Bergen has been restored to the smallest detail with much devotion and now looks exactly as in the old pictures. Bergen originally was a waterfront settlement. First came the piers and wharves, then the sheds and warehouses, and later the houses of the merchants. The streets were narrow and covered with cobblestones. The neat, often beautiful houses were marvels of woodcarving; there was always lots of timber in Norway. After the houses had burned down, been rebuilt and burned down again, it was ruled they must have no open fires. Instead fires were kept going all the time in communal cookhouses, and there the people would prepare their warm meals. Young boys watched over the fires. If

The old wooden houses by the Bryggen (*wharf*) *feature overhanging eaves, roofed gantries and chains for raising goods, wooden balconies and arcades.*

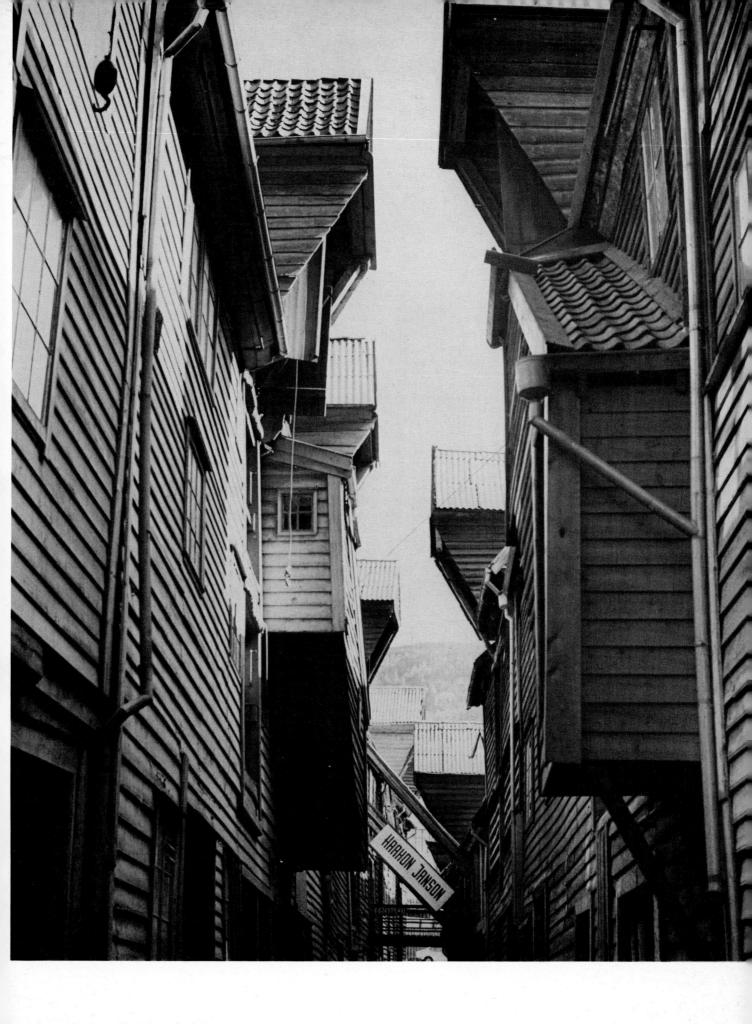

something went wrong, they used large pails that were always filled with water. The communal cookhouses, built in stone, were used by everybody, and people paid for the privilege of cooking there. They can still be visited.

How people lived in their unheated houses in wintertime is hard to understand; or perhaps we are getting too soft. Obviously people knew that internal warmth can be created by eating much food, because the habit persists today though the houses are well heated. Breakfast, known as *frokost*, was and still is an enormous meal: milk, coffee, tea, butter and cheese, hard-boiled eggs, fish (several kinds of it), cold meat, pâtés, ham, meat balls, salads and various kinds of bread. In the old days everything was cold; now there are warm dishes too, porridge and scrambled eggs and meat with sauces. Later in the day the people of Bergen would have *smörrebröd* at home, open sandwiches with nearly everything that had remained from breakfast. Around four in the afternoon there was *middag*, the hot meal cooked by the women in the communal cookhouse; soup, fish, mutton and boiled potatoes. People were rarely at home for any length of time. The men went away to catch cod and whale, and when they came back, they would prepare dried cod that was sent all over Europe, an inexpensive staple during the fasting periods in the Catholic countries. In Italy they still make many things with dried cod though they have fine fresh fish there. Today many people of Bergen fish excellent salmon from their inland waters and hunt reindeer. Salmon and reindeer dishes are the pride of Norwegian cooks.

Bergen is proud to be the hometown of Edvard Grieg, Norway's greatest composer, and of Ole Bornemann Bull, the country's most celebrated violinist. The great Henrik Ibsen lived there for some time. Grieg, born in 1843, spent many years of his life at Hop, his country home at nearby Troldhaugen, and there he wrote his music in a small wooden cabin. (On another hilltop, the modern Norwegian composer Harald Saeverud built a sturdy house of granite.)

Grieg loved his home. In March 1885 he wrote to his music publisher, Dr Max Abraham of Edition Peters in Leipzig, 'We just moved into our small villa ... I think you'll find the place heavenly. The guest room is ready, and has a wonderful view. You'll be welcome!' A few months later, Grieg wrote, 'We have a summer such as even old people cannot remember. The sky is blue and pure, except every six days, when there is a short downpour that refreshes men and nature.' But one day in December 1889 he wrote, 'The storm was so bad last night that I couldn't sleep. Only the Gods know whether we'll be able to put up with the winter.' When one visits Troldhaugen and sees the lakes, the meadows and the mountains from the isolated promontory, one understands the music of Grieg, which is really the distillate in tones of his native land. Norway's melancholy is in Grieg's music: the mysteries and folk songs, the short bright summers and the long dark nights.

Ole Bornemann Bull, born in Bergen in 1810, was a romantic fiddler like his contemporaries Sarasate and Wieniawski. His parents wanted him to become a clergyman (they rated highly in the social scale of Norway, as we know from the plays of Ibsen). Bull studied in Cassel and in 1829 heard the

The pagoda-like Fantoft stave church shows the imaginative and skilful use of timber so common in Bergen's architecture; constructed wholly of pine; it is now black from layers of preservative.

great Paganini, the greatest romantic violinist of all time. He was over-whelmed and followed Paganini to hear him as often as possible. He began to study what he thought was Paganini's technique. There was a dramatic interlude in Paris, never convincingly explained, when Bull jumped into the Seine, was rescued and 'adopted' by a wealthy woman. He imitated Paganini so well that many people who had never heard Paganini said that Ole Bull was 'better'. He died in Bergen in 1880, and his favourite violin, a very beautiful, very old Gasparo da Salò is at the Town Museum. It is decorated with ivory and bronze, and instead of a scroll it has a small angel's head and underneath a carved mermaid. According to contemporary gossip, the violin's first owner, Cardinal Aldobrandini, sent it to Benvenuto Cellini in Florence, who added the ornaments.

Since 1953 Bergen has had its own festival. There was never any doubt among Norwegians that only Bergen with its old history, beautiful landscape and northern *joie de vivre* had festival character. Some said that the Nord-land Festival might frighten people because of Bergen's rain, but then they realized that it often rains in Salzburg, in Glyndebourne and in Edinburgh, and it doesn't hurt their festivals. Actually, Bergen often has beautiful weather in May and June, known locally as 'festival weather'. The dark winter is over and everybody is happy. The programme is often first-rate. Within three weeks the Nordland Festival offers some seventy events – concerts, stage, ballet, folklore, picture shows, and at the end always a festival performance of Grieg's piano concerto in A minor. Grieg and Bergen remain the stars of the festival. 'The magic of these long days and bright nights remains the main attraction', wrote the Norwegian music critic, Hans Jörgen Hurum.

The people of Bergen agree, for they are all local patriots. They are known in Norway for their sense of humour. Ludvig Holberg, 'the Molière of the North', was born in Bergen. His famous characters, Henrik and Pernille, are drawn from his reminiscences. The people of Bergen are convinced that Bergen is the centre of the universe: they claim that the best thing in Oslo is the East Station, from which the train leaves for Bergen, and they add that 'this isn't a joke'.

INDEX

Index

Index